Offa's Dyke Circular Walks
southern section

Ian Coulthard

Published by Sigma Leisure – an imprint of
Sigma Press, 1 South Oak Lane, Wilmslow, Cheshire SK9 6AR, England.

British Library Cataloguing in Publication Data
A CIP record for this book is available from the British Library.

ISBN: 1-85058-725-6

Typesetting and Design by: Sigma Press, Wilmslow, Cheshire.

Cover photographs: The Skirrid and descent to Llanthony Priory

Cover design: MFP Design & Print

Photographs: Ian Coulthard

Maps: Morag Perrott

Printed by: MFP Design & Print

Disclaimer: the information in this book is given in good faith and is believed to be correct at the time of publication. No responsibility is accepted by either the author or publisher for errors or omissions, or for any loss or injury howsoever caused. Only you can judge your own fitness, competence and experience.

Preface

The Offa's Dyke Path was one of the first National Trails. It was established in 1971 but the route is continually evolving as diversions are established to improve the quality and safety of the walking. Latterly, the popularity of the trail has necessitated diversions or "improvement" of the path to stop increasingly severe erosion, particularly on the dyke itself. All impending diversions, of which I have been advised, have been taken into account in these walk descriptions.

The waymarking of paths on the Offa's Dyke Trail, and other long distance paths which may be utilised, is generally good whilst the level of usage tends to make the way forward obvious. It is sometimes a different matter finding the way along other connecting paths. The Offa's Dyke Path passes through ten different counties and the standard of waymarking varies between and within counties. Inspired by central government, counties are opening and waymarking all rights of way but some are making better progress than others, perhaps because they are significantly smaller in area. Volunteer groups are also active in some areas, whilst county councils have tended to give priority to the more popular walking areas. It is not surprising, therefore, to find the accessibility of paths noticeably better in the Brecon Beacons National Park and the Wye Valley (a designated Area of Outstanding Natural Beauty).

Several paths have been, or are in the process of being, reopened or diverted at my instigation. This frequently involves consultation with landowners and other interested parties and sometimes planning approval, which inevitably delays implementation. I would expect such changes to have been achieved by the time this publication is available but have also quoted the less preferable alternative route, which ensures that the circular walk can be completed.

All the walks in this guide are circular and may be started from various points on the route. The start point quoted is a compromise of the availability of readily accessible parking space and having the more energetic elements of the walk in the first few miles. There is an unusual feature of waymarking on the trail in the use of pre-cast concrete blocks and, latterly, slabs of slate referred to as "tombstones" in the National Trail Guide. I have also used "handgate" in referring to small gates, sometimes called wickets, found increasingly on bridleways to allow horseriders to pass through fences without dismounting. I have provided detailed instructions only where considered necessary though information, such as the names of houses or farms, is added as a comfort factor to reassure walkers that they are following the route correctly.

Whilst these walks are predominantly low level, the Offa's Dyke Trail undulates – not always gently. There are few walks that involve climbing over 1500 feet above sea level but the height gain may be greater. It is nonetheless relevant to take account of weather conditions both for your own comfort and safety and to avoid inconvenience to others. Always allow sufficient daylight hours to complete a walk. An allowance of one hour for each two miles plus one hour for refreshment and rest stops will be an adequate provision for regular walkers. A group leader should, however, assess the time required having regard to the abilities of the walking party.

I have been helped every step of the way by my wife, Jan, who has checked the directions by following them on each of the walks. I am also indebted to her for encouragement and enthusiasm in undertaking this project and many practical suggestions, which have improved the end product.

The companion volume of walks on the northern section of the trail will be published within a year of this book.

Ian Coulthard

Contents

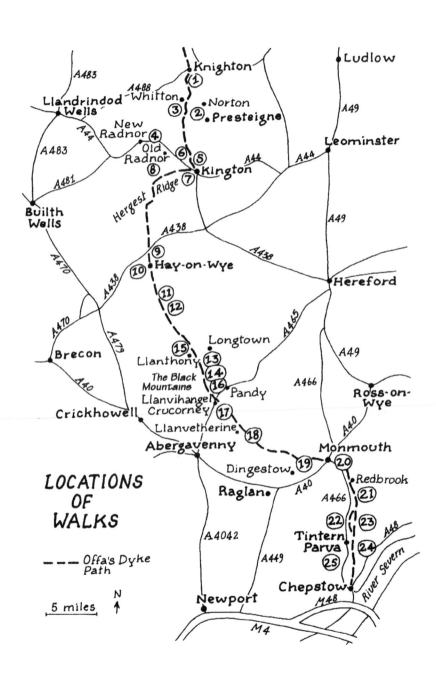

LOCATIONS
OF
WALKS

- - - Offa's Dyke
Path

5 miles

N
↑

Walk 1: Rhos-y-meirch and Glyndwr's Way from Knighton

Starting point: Grid reference 288722, car park by the bus station on the north side of Bridge Street in Knighton

Distance: 10 miles (16.1 kilometres)

Height gain: 1300 feet (400 metres)

Maps: Explorer 201 (Knighton and Presteigne), Landranger 148 (Presteigne and Hay-on-Wye)

Facilities: Full facilities in Knighton

Terrain: This walk starts with an energetic climb out of Knighton along the Offa's Dyke Trail followed by a more gradual climb over the shoulder of Rhos Hill. After descending to the A488, there is another short climb before a fairly level stretch and the gradual descent into Knighton. The walk uses mostly firm clear tracks and paths and the two long-distance trails are well waymarked. The path near the end, which contours around Garth Hill, may be muddy and can be avoided by continuing along Glyndwr's Way but this involves walking on roads for the last mile.

Knighton – in Welsh, Tref-y-Clawdd, meaning town on the dyke – is recognised as the mid-point of the Offa's Dyke Trail and there is an information centre, which walkers pass nearing the end of this walk, focussing on this long-distance trail. The footpaths officer for the trail is based there and the staff are keen to help people walking in the area.

1. Walk along Bridge Street towards the town centre and turn left up Brookside, past another car park (where payment is required). Cross Ffrydd Terrace, and follow the Offa's Dyke Path, as indicated by the finger post. Turn right behind houses and, after 50 metres, bear left up an enclosed steep path. Cross a track and take the steeper of two paths opposite as indicated by the concrete tombstone. Climb a stile and turn right alongside a wire fence at the edge of a golf course.

2. Cross a stile and continue along the right edge of fields also following the line of the dyke. At the top, where there are excellent

The Offa's Dyke Centre in Knighton

views of the surrounding countryside, the dyke also becomes more prominent. Cross the dyke and a stile in the fence on the right to continue with fence and dyke now to the left. At the end of this fine stretch of the dyke, the path veers to the right away from the fence across two fields. Pass alongside a hedge on the right and, in the next field, follow the dyke.

3. Climb a stile and turn right down a lane leaving the Offa's Dyke Trail. Turn left down another lane to a finger post and turn right up an enclosed stony bridleway also signposted to Radnor House, which continues over fields, punctuated by waymarks. Continue to follow the track steeply down into a valley and past a farmhouse.

4. At a T-junction turn right through the farmyard and follow a track up the valley. Pass a house and bear right in the next field to the diagonally opposite corner. Go through a gate joining a faint track to a farm and carry on through the farmyard along an enclosed surfaced track. Bear right at a junction and then bear

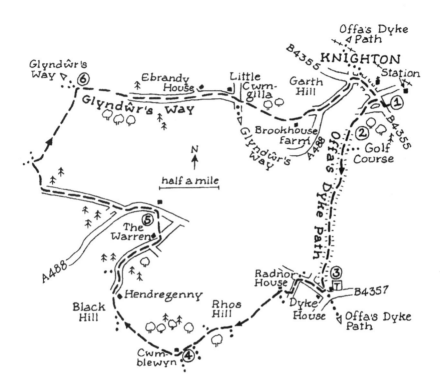

left at a junction of lanes. 100 metres further on, turn left through a gate and cross the field towards a house on the A488.

5. Cross a stile and turn left along the road for about 100 metres beyond the end of the roadside crash barrier before turning right up a minor road. 75 metres later, walk up the enclosed track ahead and gain the crest of the hill where there are glorious panoramic views. Carry on along this track passing through a sharp right-hand bend. Go through a gate and turn right to follow a fence on the right through two fields and proceed along an enclosed track. At the end of the hedge on the right and, as indicated by a finger post, turn sharply right joining Glyndwr's Way.

This long-distance trail, meandering between Knighton and Welshpool for 112 miles, passes through some of the sites of Owain Glyndwr's rebellion in the early 15th century. He formed alliances with Marcher Lords, such as the Mortimers, and the French who landed a supporting force at Milford Haven in 1405. Having previously won numerous battles in Wales, Glyndwr met an English army at Worcester and retreated. The English then pushed into Wales and Glyndwr disappeared after defeat at Harlech in 1409.

6. Follow a track down the right side of a field and then up the left side of the next field to join an enclosed track, which evolves into a surfaced lane, gradually descending towards Knighton. Cross a junction of lanes and climb over a waymarked stile, leaving Glyndwr's Way. Follow the clear path uphill for a short distance and then contour alongside a fence to the right around Garth Hill. Cross the stile ahead continuing to maintain height and pass to the left of a stone barn. Join a track, as waymarked, ascending briefly before forking right at junctions. Climb a stile and bear right to cross another stile hidden in the bottom corner of the field. Turn right down the lane to the main road and turn left to pass the Offa's Dyke Centre on the outskirts of the town.

Walk 2: The Marble Obelisk and Furrow Hill from Norton

Starting point: Grid reference 304672, park with consideration in the village of Norton

Distance: 7.5 miles (12.1 kilometres)

Height gain: 750 feet (230 metres)

Maps: Explorer 201 (Knighton and Presteigne), Landranger 148 (Presteigne and Hay-on-Wye)

Facilities: Full facilities in Presteigne and Knighton

Terrain: A gentle climb up to a ridge with good views and easy return to Norton. Generally straightforward route finding and firm ground. At the time of writing, the bridleway in paragraphs 2 and 3 is not signposted. I have confirmed the route with the County Council, but walkers should follow the waymarking which I have been assured will be installed. There are no other paths intersecting with this particular bridleway.

St Andrew's Church, in the centre of Norton, was heavily restored in Victorian times by the famous architect Sir Gilbert Scott under the sponsorship of Sir Richard Green-Price (see obelisk passed on this walk), but retaining in particular the Norman doorway.

1. Walk up Mynd Road, which is opposite the church, and turn right as waymarked after passing the last bungalow. Pass down the side of the garden and then down the road through the centre of a small modern housing development. Turn right along the main road for 75 metres and then turn left along a narrow lane for approximately half a mile.

2. Fork left at a junction and, opposite an agricultural building, bear left through a gate along a bridleway to contour across two fields. Exit the second field by way of the handgate near the bottom corner and turn left down a track to cross a stream. After walking a further 20 metres turn right across another little stream and go through a gate to climb diagonally up a field following the barely discernible bridleway. Bear right at a stand of three trees and proceed through a gate in the top corner of the

Traditionally constructed buildings, well away from the road

field. Continue in the same direction up the next field to Hill House Farm.

3. Go through a farmyard gate to pass around the left side of the long barn ahead and along a track behind the barn through two gates. Turn left up a triangular-shaped field and carry straight on up the sides of a further three fields. In the next field, bear left through a gate but continue in the same direction, now with the hedge on the right, to converge with a track leading to a road. Cross this road and walk up the lane opposite for a few metres before turning right through a gate to approach a monument in the field.

> *This well-proportioned marble obelisk is dedicated to the memory of Sir Richard Greene-Price, whose public works included establishment of the railway connecting Knighton, Llandridod Wells, Presteigne and New Radnor. He acquired Norton Manor in 1861, contributed to the renovation of the village church, and rebuilt the very substantial vicarage.*

4. Walk on to (but not across) a stile by a gate and then turn left alongside a small conifer plantation joining the Offa's Dyke

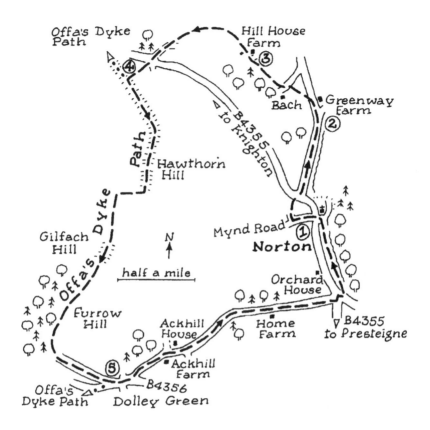

Path. Pass through another conifer plantation, crossing two stiles, and turn left to follow the dyke up Hawthorn Hill where there are exhilarating panoramic views. Soon after starting the descent, turn right as waymarked leaving the dyke. Climb over a stile at the bottom of the field and turn left alongside fencing to rejoin the dyke, though now less obvious. Now walk on to the left of the fence, looking down on the village of Whitton and the River Lugg winding along the valley, to a large finger post and bear left. After about 200 metres, join a stony track which, over the next one and a half miles, winds down to a road at Dolley Green.

5. Turn left along the road, leaving the Offa's Dyke Path and, after
passing a line of bungalows, turn left to follow a surfaced track.
Bear left around farm buildings before veering right around the
farmhouse. Go straight on for about three-quarters of a mile
along a quiet lane to cross the B4355. About 50 metres before
reaching the stream in the valley, turn left over a stile – firstly
alongside this pretty little stream then alongside conifers effec-
tively screening a sewage plant. Go forward through three
handgates and along the top of a field to cross two stiles. Walk on
to climb another stile and follow a track back to the centre of
Norton.

Walk 3: Llan-fawr and Sprigs Wood from Whitton

Starting point: Grid reference 271674, car park adjacent to St David's Church in the village of Whitton

Distance: 8.5 miles (13.7 kilometres)

Height gain: 1350 feet (420 metres)

Maps: Explorer 201 (Knighton and Presteigne), Landranger 148 (Presteigne and Hay-on-Wye)

Facilities: Full facilities in Presteigne or Knighton

Terrain: After a short walk along a quiet lane to Whitton Bridge, and then a stony track, there is a lengthy climb to open heathland. The walk then joins a track to cross a valley losing height before a short steep climb up to another ridge. Soft ground may be encountered near the River Lugg after the descent into the valley.

Whitton is a quiet hamlet spanning a road junction where there is a relatively large school. St David's Church, largely rebuilt in the late 19th century, is attractively situated and has not been surrounded by modern development. There are several noteworthy features including the 14th-century font, an older stoup (container for holy water) and 17th-century pulpit.

1. Starting from the crossroads go down the minor road to cross Whitton Bridge. Turn right along a stony waymarked track following the River Lugg upstream for a generous half-mile. Pass by a gatepost bearing waymarkers and fork left along a well-waymarked sidetrack to climb out of the valley. Go through another gate and continue uphill, leaving the track, then turn right as waymarked. After passing through a handgate, turn left and climb steeply beside a stream to emerge on open moorland. Follow the fence to the left and on attaining fairly level ground bear right (not sharp right), by a huge sycamore tree, up a faint path to the ridge.

2. Turn right just before reaching a large gorse thicket and follow the grassy track up the ridge where there are superb views across

A section of Offa's Dyke from near to the end of the walk

both valleys. Bear right to join an increasingly obvious track around the shoulder of Llan-fawr. Going through a gate the track joins a wire fence to the right and the highpoint of this track, where the trig point on top of Llan-fawr is visible, offers further glorious views. Descend towards the large conifer plantation of Forest Wood and, in the hollow by the corner of the wood, turn left down a clear track passing the large farm, Pentre.

3. Turn left along a lane, crossing a bridge, and turn right up the waymarked bridleway which is surfaced as far as Spriggs Cottage. Bear left by the cottage to continue up the enclosed bridleway and then a field to the top corner of the wood. Cross a green lane and carry on up the bridleway, which is now enclosed.

4. Pass through a gate and turn left along the top edge of four fields on an increasingly obvious track. Keep left of a cluster of agricultural buildings and go through a gate to continue in the same direction on the left of a young conifer plantation. Turn right along

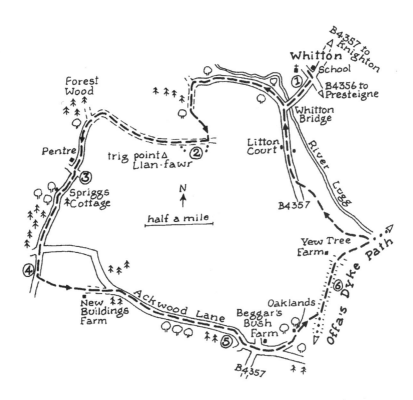

Ackwood Lane, a green lane initially somewhat overgrown that runs along the ridge for about a mile before dropping down to a lane.

5. Turn left, cross the B4357, and walk up the narrow lane opposite passing Beggars Bush Farm. About 150 metres further on turn left along a track, passing to the right of Oaklands, and cross a stream. Contour across three fields and through the intervening gates admiring the view towards Whitton. Approaching two gates pass through the one on the right, cross the dyke, and turn left down the Offa's Dyke Trail.

> *The trail at this point follows a particularly prominent section of the dyke which, unusually, is not covered with trees and other vegetation.*

6. Cross a stile, bear left down a track beside the dyke, and cross the adjacent stile in the bottom corner of the field. Climb over the stile on the opposite side of the lane and continue alongside a ditch to the River Lugg, where the walk leaves the Offa's Dyke Trail. Turn sharp left away from the river to cross the stile in the middle of the fence ahead. Go straight on as waymarked over the next field to cross a cluster of stiles and a footbridge. Follow the hedge along the left side of the next field, pass through the gate to the right of a copse, and contour across the next field to climb a stile. Proceed along the left side of a field to a marker post then bear slightly left up to the corner of the field. Climb the stile and turn right along a lane to Whitton Bridge and the village.

Walk 4: Ditchyeld Bridge and Evenjobb from New Radnor

Starting point: Grid reference 214607, park with consideration in the village

Distance: 12.5 miles (20.1 kilometres)

Height gain: 1500 feet (460 metres)

Maps: Explorer 201 (Knighton and Presteigne), Landranger 148 (Presteigne and Hay-on-Wye)

Facilities: Facilities in New Radnor

Terrain: A particularly fine stretch of the trail following the dyke for over a mile and the open heathland of Bache Hill connected by green lanes and field paths. The ground is generally firm and route finding mostly very straightforward.

Paragraph 3 refers to proceeding down a lane and turning left along a road to Ditchyeld Bridge, in the process of which, joining the Offa's Dyke Trail. The County Council is opening the right of way from the lane, providing a path through fields parallel to the road, to emerge near Ditchyeld Bridge. I hope that there will also soon be a permitted path following a more direct route alongside the brook. Walkers should therefore follow waymarking to the left, when it has been put in place, after crossing the brook but before reaching the road.

New Radnor was established in the 13th century beneath the castle, which was destroyed by Owain Glyndwr in 1401 when he was carrying all before him. The grid plan of the streets suggests an initially substantial settlement, which failed to develop in competition with Presteigne. The most obvious feature in the town is the memorial to Sir George Cornewall Lewis, a Chancellor of the Exchequer in Victorian times.

1. Walk downhill past the memorial on the south side of the town, towards the A44 bypass, and turn left down a lane soon passing a school. This lane deteriorates to a generally enclosed and straight track to be followed for about one and a half miles. At a road junction, the walk continues along the lane ahead, but detour 60 metres along the lane to the right to see the Four Stones.

The Four Stones to the right of the track

This is the only known example in Wales of a style of prehistoric monument more frequently seen in Scotland. There are numerous tumuli in the area and in the next one and a half miles the path passes near the sites of a Roman fort and Motte and Bailey type of castle.

2. Return to the road junction and turn right along the lane to continue in the same direction for another half-mile. At the next road junction carry straight on through a gate and go up the right side of fields. Go forward along an increasingly obvious track now with a hedge to the left. At a junction of tracks, bear right and soon join a lane bending right past farm buildings and Womaston School.

3. Cross the bridge over a brook and continue down the lane (but see comments under terrain above regarding a footpath which is not accessible at the time of writing). Turn left down the road to the old Ditchyeld Bridge, joining the Offa's Dyke Trail by a farm.

N.B. NORTH IS NOT AT THE TOP OF THIS MAP!

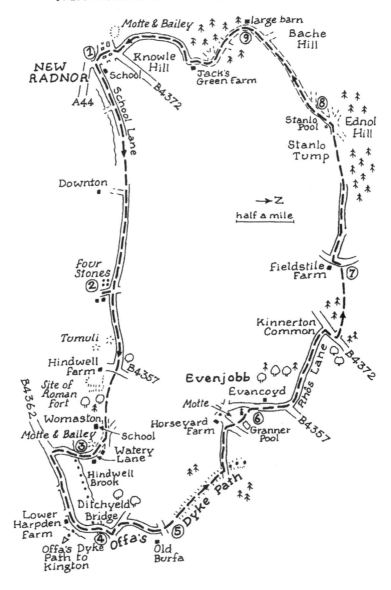

4. Turn left along a narrow lane, as indicated by the finger post, for about 200 metres then bear right up a track into woodland. Go straight on at the next junction and pass the magnificent late-medieval farmstead of Old Burfa. Turn left down a lane for 50 metres and then turn right to climb a stile and steps. Continue along the top of a bank which is, of course, Offa's Dyke.

> *This is possibly the most impressive section of the dyke with the ditch still evident and demonstrating the classic defensive position above open ground climbing increasingly steeply to the dyke.*

5. Walk beside or along the dyke as directed for the next mile before leaving the Offa's Dyke Trail, turning left down a lane into the hamlet of Evenjobb. Turn right at a road junction and, almost immediately, turn left through a waymarked handgate to pass through a cottage garden. Go straight on through another gate and over stiles towards the church.

> *Best viewed from the village, a quarter of a mile away, St Peter's Church is an unremarkable Victorian building though the spire will frequently be in view during the walk.*

6. After crossing the stile adjacent to the church bear right to the road by way of another stile and turn right. 50 metres after passing the entrance to Evancoyd, bear left down a byway. Fork left in the hollow to cross the footbridge over a stream and go through a gate where the surface of the track deteriorates significantly. Continue along this track for a generous half-mile to a road and turn right briefly before turning left through the next field gate. Walk up a large field past a telegraph pole, then bear left along the side of a small conifer plantation, and go ahead up the next two fields to another lane.

7. Turn left along this lane for 130 metres and then turn right up a surfaced track. At a junction of bridleways by a marker post fork left to follow a very straight track steadily uphill. Pass through gates along the bottom side of a large forest for about a mile. Go through the handgate ahead to a forest track and a junction of paths at a place called Stanlo Pool (although there is no pool in evidence now).

8. Turn left through another handgate onto open moorland following the obvious track ahead, climbing more gradually than before and enjoying the wide-ranging panoramas before starting the descent to New Radnor. Pass through a gate as a large barn comes into view ahead and 75 metres further on cross a stile to the left and continue in the same direction.

9. Cross another stile to rejoin the track at the top corner of woodland near the barn and then take the next left turn down a grassy track. Cross a forest road and walk on down a narrow path to cross the same forest road at a lower level. Carry on down a clearer path along the bottom of the forestry. Pass to the left of a small pool and, at a T-junction of paths, turn right to soon join an enclosed track to New Radnor. Turn left down a lane, right at crossroads and left again down the main street of the town.

Walk 5: The Mortimer Trail from Kington

Starting point: Grid reference 295567, The Square at the top end of the main street (Church Street) by the Swan Hotel

Distance: 11 miles (17.7 kilometres)

Height gain: 1300 feet (400 metres)

Maps: Explorer 201 (Knighton and Presteigne), Landranger 148 (Presteigne and Hay-on-Wye)

Facilities: Full facilities in Kington

Terrain: Mostly field paths across well-drained grassland and incorporating a long but not energetic climb in the first part of the walk and later a fairly steep climb up to walk along Offa's Dyke. Signposting is generally good with most of the walk utilising two long-distance trails.

The Offa's Dyke Trail passes through Kington and the Mortimer Trail ends there helping to promote the town as a walking centre. The traditional high street has been retained at the top of which is the historic church with the castle mound nearby. The Mortimer Trail, established in the 1990's and only 30 miles long, passes through the border country between Ludlow and Kington. The Mortimers, from whom King Edward IV was descended, were powerful Marcher Lords based at Wigmore and Ludlow.

1. Leave The Square by way of the passageway on the right side of the Garth Nursing Home, joining the Mortimer Trail. Turn left at a junction of passages and carry straight on at subsequent junctions to emerge onto a pavement. Turn left along another narrow passageway, behind a garage and parallel to the road, at the end of which, turn right to a roundabout on the bypass. Bear left up the Titley road and turn right down a waymarked track by "The Far Patch". Walk straight on down the side of fields and then bear left at a marker post by an isolated sycamore tree, following overhead cables, to cross the stile ahead. Continue in the same direction to cross a footbridge and stile before turning left down a farm track.

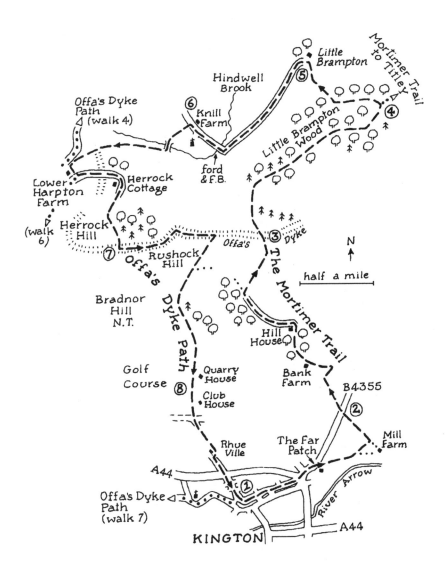

2. Cross a road, the stile ahead and the ensuing field to the diagonally opposite corner. Turn right along the bottom edge of the next field before turning sharply left to join a track up towards a farm. Bear right to circumvent the farm and rejoin the track still going uphill. Cross a stile and leave this track to walk straight on down a field with a hedge to the right. Bear right across a lane to proceed up the narrow lane ahead for about a half-mile, at the end of which bear right below the gorse to climb Rushock Hill. Cross a stile about 100 metres higher than the end of the sparse hedge ahead and continue in the same direction to the marker post on the skyline. Bear left as waymarked up to Offa's Dyke, which runs down the spine of the hill.

3. Walk on past the marker post on the dyke and, on nearing a conifer plantation, join a grassy track. Cross a stile to carry on along the track to the bottom corner of the next field and then along the edge of woodland. Turn right along another track for about 100 metres and then turn right by a marker post to follow a path for over half a mile up the edge of the woods. Emerge from the woodland to pass along the right side of a field and, at a junction of paths, turn left down a green lane for about 250 metres. Bear right to cross a stile and walk along the top side of a field for 50 metres then turn left across the green lane, leaving the Mortimer Trail.

4. Bear right in the next field to follow a waymarked track descending obliquely through woodland. At the bottom end of the woods, turn right over a stile to walk down the middle of a large field and then alongside a hedge to the right. Where this hedge finishes, bear right to reach a green lane by a farm.

Note the resplendent 16th-century timber-framed farmhouse – an outbuilding near the path incorporates a stone tablet which reads "Johan Robinson handstructured edifice AD 1687".

5. Turn left to follow the lane for nearly a mile and, shortly after passing through a gate, follow the lane bending right to a ford. Cross the adjacent footbridge and walk on down the lane to pass magnificent farmhouses in the hamlet of Knill.

Consider a short detour along the lane to the left to see the very attractively situated St Michael's Church, which dates from Norman times.

6. Turn left through a field gate, as waymarked, and walk towards the top of Herrock Hill, visible in the distance. Pass through another gate and bear right around the gardens of a country house to a substantial footbridge over Hindwell Brook. Turn right to walk parallel to the meandering brook and across three fields towards the right side of a farm. In the process cross the barely discernible Offa's Dyke forming the hedge line between the second and third fields. Turn left along a track by the farm, joining the Offa's Dyke Trail, and where this track bends left cross the stile ahead before bearing left to a handgate. Turn left up a track, through a gate and over stiles, bearing right progressively to climb Herrock Hill.

7. At a junction of paths on the ridge, indicated by a finger post, turn left and continue climbing more gradually to join the line of the dyke. Turn right by the second finger post on the dyke (ignoring the path ahead which provides a link to the Mortimer Trail) to start the descent into Kington. In the next field walk beside the hedge to the left before diverging from it to cross a stile and veer left to contour across the following field. Climb a stile under a large oak tree and bear left, climbing slightly, along a clearer path to cross another stile and the top corner of a field. Carry on towards a strip of mature woodland and bear right. In the next field bear right to go through the gate in the diagonally opposite corner and briefly join a surfaced track.

8. Bear left down a grassy path diverging from another surfaced track to cross the golf course. Cross a fairway, being aware of golfers playing in the vicinity, to pass down the right side of a whitewashed stone cottage. Bear left to pass between another two cottages and follow the obvious path, either enclosed or straight down fields. Turn left down a lane to cross the bypass and footbridge opposite. Bear left up a lane past a terrace of attractively maintained cottages and straight up to The Square.

Walk 6: Herrock Hill from Kington

Starting point: Grid reference 295567, The Square at the top end of the main street (Church Street) by the Swan Hotel

Distance: 7.5 miles (12.1 kilometres)

Height gain: 750 feet (230 metres)

Maps: Explorer 201 (Knighton and Presteigne), Landranger 148 (Presteigne and Hay-on-Wye)

Facilities: Full facilities in Kington

Terrain: Clear paths and tracks excepting for the approach to Kington at the end of the walk. There is just one fairly long climb at the start of the walk; ground conditions are generally good.

Kington is one of the six market towns of Herefordshire with a long history as a Marcher border town. Although the town is small there is a good range of facilities and it makes an excellent touring centre.

1. Leave The Square at the top right-hand corner, passing the old National School building and immediately joining the Offa's Dyke Trail. Where Llewelyn Road bends right, walk straight on down the cul-de-sac called Crooked Well. Cross a footbridge and the by-pass to start climbing the lane opposite as indicated by a finger post. Just before reaching a farmyard, turn right through a handgate to join an enclosed track up the right side of the farmhouse. Go through a kissing gate and walk on up the field, through another kissing gate to join an enclosed footpath. Emerging onto open heathland by a finger post bear left up a broad grassy path to another finger post and then veer right to climb more steeply. Cross a fairway of the golf course, noting the warning sign, and continue in the same direction to a handgate by the cattle-grid.

    The golf course is on National Trust land and is the highest in England peaking at 1284 feet above sea level.

2. Join a surfaced track briefly before forking left along a grassy track which later diverges from the outer perimeter of the golf course. Cross a stile in the top corner of the field and pass to the

left of a copse of oak trees. As the field opens out, bear left to contour across to, and over, a stile. Go straight on to the next stile and contour across the ensuing field. Pass to the left of a large oak tree and again contour across the next field to climb the stile in the top corner. Converge progressively with the fence to the right and cross one more stile before bearing left towards the finger post soon visible on the skyline.

Do not cross the stile on the ridge – this gives access to a link path to the Mortimer Trail (see walk 5).

3. Turn left along the ridge and Offa's Dyke crossing two stiles before descending along a clear grassy path. Cross another stile by a gate and 30 metres later bear left along the narrower path. At a T-junction of paths turn right* (turning left at this point shortens the walk by about a mile and a half), as indicated by a finger post and shortly after ignore the more prominent uphill path. Descend the side of Herrock Hill, crossing two stiles.

4. Approaching a gate and stile bear left above a cottage, leaving the Offa's Dyke Trail. Contour alongside the fence at the top of

Harvest time below Herrock Hill

the field system. After about a half-mile turn left up a clear grassy track, alongside the same fence, until confronted by a fence. The nearby finger post indicates the path descending from the left, which provides the optional short-cut*. Climb the stile ahead and bear right to cross another stile. Veer right, as waymarked, to join a track descending along the valley between Herrock Hill and Bradnor Hill.

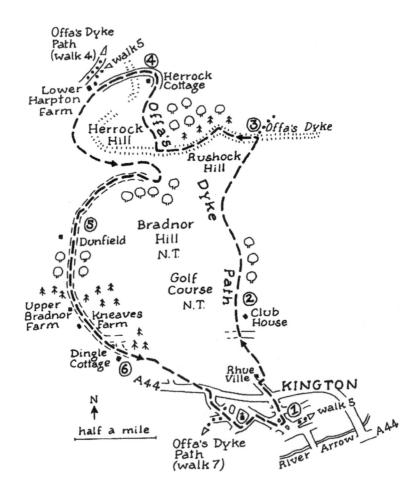

5. In the field before reaching a farm bear left along the bank above the stream. Climb a stile and walk straight on along an increasingly prominent path. Cross a field, climbing slightly, to pass through a waymarked gate into woodland. Almost immediately fork left, then 30 metres further on fork right as waymarked and bear right at the next intersection to go on inside the edge of the woodland. Pass a house and go briefly uphill before forking right at a marker post. Go through a handgate and bear left along a broad grassy track. Pass through a gate and turn right down a lane to Dingle Cottage.

6. Turn left opposite the cottage and contour across fields along a faint path and then climb to pass alongside the driveway of a large stone cottage. Cross two adjacent stiles and follow the fence down to the right to go through a gate before turning left along a tarmac drive. Leave the drive to cross the stile in view ahead. Bear right down the next two fields and pass through the gate in the bottom corner, at the junction of the Kington road with the A44. Walk up the Kington road, past the church, and down Church Road.

Walk 7: Hergest Ridge and Huntington from Kington

Starting point: Grid reference 295567, The Square at the top end of the main street (Church Street) by the Swan Hotel

Distance: 10 miles (16.1 kilometres)

Height gain: 1150 feet (350 metres)

Maps: Explorer 201 (Knighton and Presteigne), Landranger 148 (Presteigne and Hay-on-Wye)

Facilities: Full facilities in Kington, public house in Huntington

Terrain: An easy climb onto Hergest Ridge along clear firm tracks. There is no clear path on the descent, and the remainder of the walk uses some low-lying field paths where the ground is likely to be soft. Route-finding in the latter half of the walk is not always straightforward. A few short stretches of path may be overgrown but there is a very active footpath preservation society based in Kington whose members clear such overgrown paths periodically.

Kington, probably derived from Kingtown, in pre-Norman times centred around the castle and church. In the late 13th century, it developed as Kington in the Fields and was situated below St Mary's Church (Early English style) that is passed at the start of the walk. It is quite a busy little market town with a good range of shops.

1. Turn right up Church Street, which extends into Church Road, passing the church and joining the Offa's Dyke Trail. Where Church Road descends to the A44, turn left up a lane signposted to Hergest Croft to pass the gardens, as the lane deteriorates to a rough track.

    The gardens of Hergest Croft are amongst the finest in the country extending over 50 acres and worth a visit, possibly combined with refreshments, at the end of the walk.

2. Go through a gate onto Hergest Ridge taking the left of two stony tracks, which soon becomes a broad grassy path climbing gently. Ignore the left fork towards the fencing and, approaching the crest of the ridge, pass a marker post where the old race-

course intersects the bridleway and an enclosure of mon-
key-puzzle trees.

*Detour to the right towards two footpath marker posts to see the
Whet Stone and then return to the Offa's Dyke Trail. This name is
said to originate from a procedure developed during times of
plague, such as the Black Death, when farmers left their wheat on
the stone and retired to a safe distance for buyers to take the wheat
and leave their payment. It has also been suggested that the granite
block was actually used as a whetstone.*

The Whet Stone on Hergest Ridge

3. Follow the path bending gradually left towards the trig point to
pass a small pool. 200 metres further on at a finger post indicating a junction of paths turn left leaving the Offa's Dyke Trail.

4. This path is not clear and there are few features of significance
on the ridge. Pass to the right of the trig point before passing a
marker post. Continue in the same direction downhill towards
the left-hand edge of a large plantation on the opposite hillside,
if necessary bearing right of the impenetrable gorse thickets. On
reaching a finger post just above the top fences of the field sys-

tem (where a stone wall and fence converge to a field gate) turn right to continue walking along the open hillside. Stay alongside the fence at the top end of the field system, which at one point involves ascending briefly, and join a track curving around a hollow. About 150 metres further on, converge with the fence and turn left through a waymarked gate to follow an enclosed bridleway downhill between farm buildings onto a surfaced track.

5. Turn left along this track and then turn right through the next field gate to continue downhill, to the right of mature trees, to a lane. Bear right across the lane and resume the downhill route along an enclosed path before crossing a footbridge to go up fields parallel to the hedges to the right. Turn right up a farm track for 50 metres and then turn left through a gate. Pass through the gate in the far corner of the field and go to the left of the barn ahead. Turn left along a lane and then right along a footpath, past Rock Cottage, beside a stream. Turn left up a surfaced cross-track to pass around two sides of the mound and fortifications of Huntington Castle (unfortunately, nothing remains of the castle). Cross the next road junction and turn right opposite the Swan Inn to the church.

The distance between the castle and the church suggests a far larger settlement than exists today. In the 13th century, the Normans attempted to establish a new border town here to replace Kington, which obviously failed. The very handsome church of St Thomas à Beckett dates from the 13/14th centuries, the original building having been reputedly erected as a penance by one of his murderers.

6. Turn left through two kissing gates in front of the church and cross a stile to go along the right side of two fields. Cross a stile and pass the nearby cottage to cross a lane and continue in the same direction over fields with hedges to the left. Pass to the left of a small pond and keep to the left of a stream to cross a stile and another large field. Go through a handgate and across the top corner of woodland for just 50 metres. Turn right along the edge

N.B. NORTH IS NOT AT THE TOP OF THIS MAP!

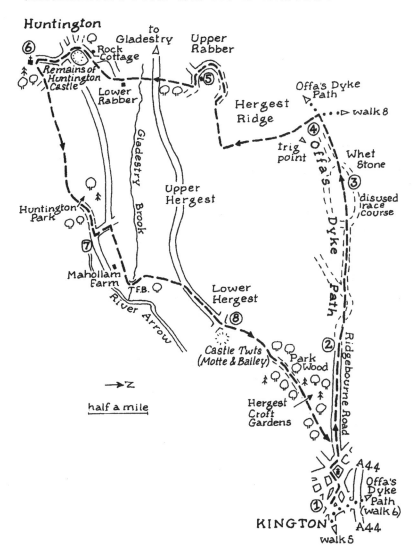

of fields joining a track, which bends right to reach a lane at a sharp bend.

7. Turn left up the lane to the next bend and turn right through a gate to walk down the ridge of a large field. Pass a farm and bear right to go through a waymarked gate and forward to cross two stiles in quick succession before turning left along a concrete track. Follow the fence to the left to cross a footbridge and then bear left up two fields. Cross a stile, walk diagonally up two fields to join an enclosed track and turn right along a lane into the hamlet of Lower Hergest. Go forward as waymarked at a road junction briefly along a track, cross the stile on the right and follow the fence to the left into a hollow.

> *The mound to the right is the sight of Castle Twts – a minor stronghold that was probably constructed of timber rather than stone.*

8. Bear left to cross a footbridge and stile and walk up the left side of fields crossing numerous stiles. Bear right across a long rectangular field to enter Park Wood by way of a stile. Follow the main track through this landscaped woodland and, having emerged from the woods but before reaching the finger post ahead, turn left up the bank to another finger post by a gate. Go through the gate and contour across a field (ignoring the white marker posts) with Hergest Croft Gardens to the left. Cross the stile ahead, pass through a kissing gate and a field gate before bearing left around the elevated gardens of a mansion to a lane, crossing the driveway in the process. Turn right and right again down Church Road into Kington.

Walk 8: Gladestry and Hergest Ridge from Old Radnor

Starting point: Grid reference 250591, car park opposite St Stephen's Church, in the village of Old Radnor

Distance: 8 miles (12.9 kilometres)

Height gain: 1300 feet (380 metres)

Maps: Explorer 201 (Knighton and Presteigne), Landranger 148 (Presteigne and Hay-on-Wye)

Facilities: Public house in Old Radnor and Gladestry, full facilities in Kington

Terrain: Mostly well-drained tracks and paths, though short boggy stretches may be encountered. There are several ascents, most notably on leaving Gladestry up to Hergest Ridge. Route finding is a bit tricky in places where there are no reassuring waymarkers.

Old Radnor was superseded by New Radnor about 1250 and is now a sleepy hamlet. It is dominated by a fine and exceptionally large church, rebuilt in the 15/16th centuries after being burnt by Owain Glyndwr in 1401 (when the church was English), though many features dating back to earlier medieval times have survived. There is a massive crudely carved pre-Norman font, which originally may have been a Celtic altar-stone. The nearby inn, beautifully situated, is 17th century and has lately been sympathetically restored and re-opened.

1. Turn left out of the car park and right at the road junction to circumvent the church before bearing left at the next bend to follow a narrow lane also waymarked as a footpath. Carry on down this lane around the left side of a farm after which the lane deteriorates to a rough track. Continue to follow this track along the left side of a field, through two gates enclosing an old railway track bed, and on to a lane. Turn right to the next bend and turn left to pass to the right of a cottage through a handgate, over two stiles and a footbridge – all in quick succession. Proceed through two fields by the hedge to the right and then join an enclosed track leading to a lane.

Village pub in Old Radnor

2. Turn right along the lane for about 200 metres, past Penlan and a farm, before turning left over a waymarked stile. Bear left to follow a sunken path, at the end of which climb a stile and bear left through the garden of a cottage down to a track in the valley. Turn sharp right along this grassy track and carry on in the same direction across a long field. Join a track crossing the stream and winding up the other side of the valley to a farm, forking left as waymarked at a junction of tracks.

3. Turn left through the farmyard and take the left-hand of two gates to follow a track bending left around a copse. Cross the field ahead passing to the left of a large isolated oak tree and then turn right up the bank to cross a stile. Go up the left side of the next field and then proceed in the same direction to a cottage. Join a track from the cottage to a farm and cross the stile ahead to go forward initially down a sunken track. The path then follows the hedges on the right down to Gladestry.

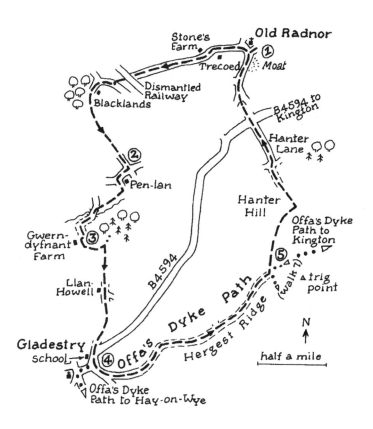

St Mary's Church at the far end of the village, past the Royal Oak and houses dating from the 16th century, is worth a detour. The nave is 13th century (as are the piscina and stoup in the sanctuary), and the church was enlarged in the 14th century, with a tower dating from the 15th century. The roofs are mainly 15/16th century and, whilst there have been further additions and renovations excepting in Victorian times, the overall impression is very pleasing.

4. Go down the road past the school and, on the bend, turn left up a lane to join the Offa's Dyke Trail. Fork left at the next junction to commence the steep climb up to Hergest Ridge. After passing through two gates the surface of the lane deteriorates to a track. As this track levels out pass a marker post and, 100 metres further on, take the middle of three paths noting further marker posts ahead. Pass by a small pool and then keep left along the more prominent path to a finger post indicating a cross-track.

5. Turn left, leaving the Offa's Dyke Trail, in the direction of Hanter Hill and descend to the corner of a conifer plantation where several paths meet. Go forward for about 40 metres and pass a marker post (also indicating another footpath to the right) to go over the right shoulder of Hanter Hill. Follow this path downhill joining a fence to the right and later an enclosed track. About 150 metres before reaching another track at the base of Hanter Hill, turn right to a farm and then bear left down the farm lane to a road. Cross the road and walk straight on before turning left over a footbridge 20 metres after passing a letterbox. Go up a field to the right of the farm and cross a stile. Climb up the next field keeping to the right of a stream, and then turn right along a lane into Old Radnor.

Walk 9: Whitney Toll Bridge from Hay-on-Wye

Starting point: Grid reference 229423, car park by the information centre in Hay-on-Wye

Distance: 13.5 miles (21.7 kilometres)

Height gain: 1050 feet (350 metres)

Maps: Explorer 201 (Knighton and Presteigne), Landranger 148 (Presteigne and Hay-on-Wye)

Facilities: Full facilities in Hay-on-Wye

Terrain: A mixture of field paths, tracks and country lanes. The routes of both the Offa's Dyke Trail and the Wye Valley Walk are somewhat complex in this area but are generally adequately waymarked. The going may be soft in places. The River Wye is prone to flooding which may result in riverside paths being impassable. If in doubt, check with Hay-on-Wye information centre.

Hay-on-Wye is now a busy little town, prosperity having returned with the second-hand book trade and the increasing popularity of outdoor pursuits in the surrounding countryside. The Normans established a motte and bailey castle near St Mary's Church on the south-west side of the border town but the castle in the centre was established circa 1200. The Marcher Lords occupying the castle were variously attacked by both Welsh Chieftains and English Monarchs but the castle was rebuilt numerous times, the last occasion being in the 17th century as a Jacobean mansion.

1. Turn left out of the car park, joining the Offa's Dyke Trail, and turn right briefly along Castle Street, bear left down Belmont Road, then turn left down Bridge Street to cross the River Wye. Turn right at a finger post and fork left a few yards later to join the obvious path through woodland beside the river. Continue ahead across fields where the path very gradually diverges from the riverbank. Cross a stile about 100 metres away from the river and go forward with a hedge to the left. Turn left briefly along a track and then turn right by a finger post along an enclosed bridleway. At the end of this path cross the stile on the right and

Toll-keeper's cottage at Whitney Bridge

continue along the edge of fields with a hedge to the left. Climb a stile beside a gate and cross the next field to pass to the right of farm buildings. Bear left around the farm and walk on across two fields. Cross a stile/footbridge combination and follow the stream for a short distance before bearing left to climb up to the road.

2. Turn right along the road for about 300 metres and then turn left up a narrow lane passing a reassuring trail finger post. After a short steep climb bear left over a stile and climb though woodland along a broad winding path. Fork right, as waymarked along the top edge of the woods, and then go up a broad rocky track through the woodland. Bear left at a junction of paths along a fairly level path before a short climb to emerge on a narrow lane.

3. Turn right and after about a quarter of a mile, at crossroads, turn right along another lane for a further quarter-mile before bearing left over a well-signposted stile. Walk up fields towards the farm, which soon comes into view before turning left along a lane past the farm. Turn right up an enclosed track by Pen-y-van and at the end of this bridleway turn right along a lane, leaving the Offa's Dyke Trail.

4. Turn right along a track, signposted to Penbrilley Farm, which bends left then right. Cross a cattle-grid into the farmyard and immediately turn left alongside a hedge and shortly cross a waymarked stile. Go straight on to cross a stile in the corner of the next field and carry on with hedges to the left. Descend between a hedge and a wire fence towards a stream and then turn right to walk along the valley. Bear right along a track past a barn and go through the left-hand gate ahead to cross two fields diagonally to a lane by Upper Bridge Court. Bear left around this property and follow the narrow lane past Lower Bridge Court to a T-junction. Turn left and, about 300 metres later, turn right down a track and turn right at the next junction to shortly pass through a handgate. Bear left, slightly uphill, along a faint path for about 200 metres to a junction of tracks. Go straight on as waymarked down the track ahead and descend to the A438 by the toll bridge over the River Wye.

Whitney-on-Wye Toll Bridge was first established in 1774 to replace the ferry crossing 200 metres downstream. This bridge fell in one of the frequent floods as did the subsequent two, all stone built, over a period of only 20 years. These were then replaced by the present design, partly timber construction, which has withstood the floodwaters. Sympathetic renovation has been undertaken in recent years and, together with the tollgate cottage, is a very attractive and photogenic scene. Picnic tables in the lay-by also make this an obvious lunch stop.

5. Go over the bridge (no charge for pedestrians!) and carry on along the road for some 400 metres and then turn left over a waymarked stile to cross a large field towards the house of a large farm. Enter the unusually tidy and attractive farmyard by way of a sturdy wrought iron gate and pass straight through to bear right across two fields. 20 metres after passing a field gate in the far corner of the second field cross a stile/bridge combination and walk up the left side of the next field to cross a stile in the top corner. Follow a clear path winding uphill through woodland. Pass along the side of a house and cross a lane to climb up the waymarked path opposite, again in woodland. This path becomes increasingly indistinct when passing

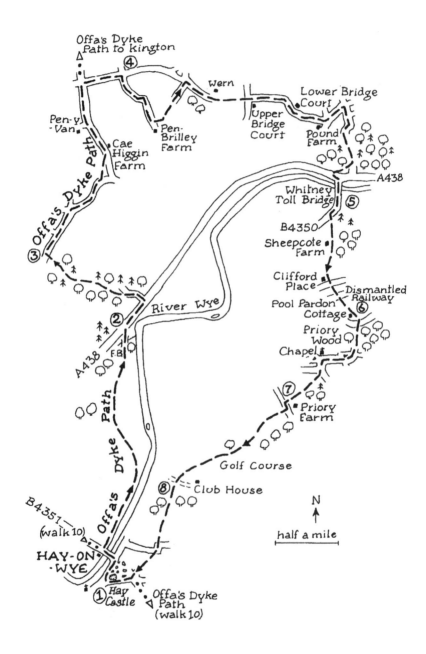

through bracken in the height of the summer but soon reaches a dismantled railway line in a shallow cutting. Stiles and steps are provided to cross the cutting before climbing steeply up a field past a large tree. Go through a field gate adjacent to a telegraph pole as waymarked where there are superb views looking back over the Wye Valley. Continue in the same direction through fields and turn right to pass down the side of Pool Pardon Cottage, cross a lane and join the Wye Valley Walk.

This trail winds through the countryside, generally following the River Wye, for 112 miles between Rhayader and Chepstow.

6. Walk on alongside a fence, cross a stile/bridge combination to continue into the village of Priory Wood. Cross a triangle of open ground and turn right along a lane to pass a dilapidated Methodist chapel on the outskirts of the village. Turn left at the T-junction and, at the junction of three lanes, go straight on down an enclosed path. Bear right to cross a field and stile then bear left to join a track down the side of the field before turning left along another lane.

7. Turn right, opposite a farm, along a stony track (ignoring the handgate to the right) through several fields alongside a hedge. Cross a stream by way of a footbridge and follow the track into a large field to walk on, with a hedge to the left. Where the hedge bends left, go straight on. Cross a stile onto a golf course and bear right to follow marker posts (if in doubt bear right towards the edge of the course to find the next marker post and be aware of golfers playing nearby).

8. Leave the golf course by way of a stile a few hundred metres downhill from the clubhouse to cross a paddock and small belt of woodland. Pass through a succession of fields in a fairly straight line, where the ensuing waymarked stile is generally in view, to join a lane. 100 metres later, where the lane bends sharply right, walk straight on and bear right to cross a quaint little stone clapper bridge in a hollow. Bear right across the remaining fields to pass over a footbridge before a short climb along a track into Hay-on-Wye. Turn left by the Olde Black Lion Inn and right at the T-junction to return to the car park.

Walk 10: Glasbury from Hay-on-Wye

Starting point: Grid reference 229423, car park by the information centre in Hay-on-Wye

Distance: 11 miles (17.7 kilometres)

Height gain: 900 feet (270 metres)

Maps: Outdoor Leisure 13 (Brecon Beacons National Park – East), Landranger 161 (Abergavenny and Black Mountains)

Facilities: Full facilities in Hay-on-Wye, limited facilities including toilets in Glasbury and public house in Llowes

Terrain: Very largely field paths and route finding often requires careful attention. Two stretches of the Wye Valley Walk utilised in the latter third of the walk are along the A438 – beware fast-moving traffic. The River Wye is prone to flooding which may make the paths along the river bank impassable. If in doubt, check at Hay-on-Wye information centre.

The border town of Hay-on-Wye has had an eventful history but in the 20th century had become drab with little to attract the visitor. It has slowly been regenerated as a major centre of the second-hand book trade and is also developing as a centre for outdoor pursuits including walking. The town is now increasingly prosperous and colourful. It has a weekly market and, additionally, various fairs and a festival of literature early in the summer. In the centre the early 13th-century castle has been partially restored whilst the narrow winding streets are best explored on foot, leaving the car in a huge car park by the information centre.

1. Turn right out of the car park and turn right down a track immediately after passing a doctors' surgery, joining the Offa's Dyke Trail. Walk straight on through fields passing through kissing gates. Cross the footbridge over a stream and follow the obvious path uphill climbing the intervening stiles. Bear right as indicated by a marker post to cross a stile and turn left along a lane (there is a proposal to divert the Offa's Dyke Trail from the marker post to emerge higher up the lane).

2. Pass through a dip in the lane and turn right over a stile to walk

along the bank of a stream. Cross the stream by way of a foot-bridge when abreast of the house to the left and follow the stream up the opposite bank. Cross a stile and continue up another field to turn right along an enclosed surfaced track, leaving the Offa's Dyke Trail.

3. Follow this track through the small farmstead of Upper Danyforest and up to a left-hand bend. Walk straight on across Hen Allt Common as indicated by the marker post (ignoring a stile to the right). Follow a clear winding path climbing gradually and pass through a clearing with splendid views over Hay in the valley below. Contour along the hill before climbing again briefly, as indicated by another marker post, to go straight through a farmyard and turn right down a lane. Where this lane bends right for the second time, bear left across a waymarked stile beside a gate and follow an initially faint track along the top side of a field. The track then winds past Long Cairn commencing the gradual descent to Glasbury.

A small rectangular chamber constructed out of stone slabs is the only obvious feature of this Neolithic tomb, excavated in the 1920s, which extends to the west of the path.

The only obvious feature of Long Cairn

4. At a junction of tracks continue along a clearer stony track winding downhill and turn right down a lane for a short distance.
Cross the stile on the left and walk down towards the village of
Llanigon. Pass a stile on the right giving access to a lane and
walk on through mature trees, descending steeply, to cross a
stile well hidden in the corner of the field. Go down the clear
path to a kissing gate, cross the footbridge by a ford and follow
the lane into Llanigon.

Bear right through the churchyard to see the attractive St Eigen's
Church which dates from Norman times although mainly from the
15th-17th centuries. Note the ancient font and quern in the porch.

5. Leave the churchyard by the gate in the opposite corner from the
point of entry to turn right down the lane. Cross the main road
and go down the track opposite to pass through Llanthomas
Farm. Continue in the same direction in the next field, turning
left by a pole to go through a gate and join a track along the top of
two fields before crossing a third field in the same direction. In
the next two fields bear right towards a bungalow by the farm in
the hollow. Pass through a small paddock between the bungalow and farm to a junction of tracks, then turn right to wind between the farm buildings as indicated by a nature trail sign. Bear
left down an enclosed track, past the imposing early 17th-cen-
tury farmhouse. Keep to the main track, which bends left to contour above a belt of woodland, for a generous half-mile. Follow
the track down through the woods and soon cross a footbridge to
emerge at a junction of three lanes.

6. Bear right for half a mile to pass a farm on the right and then
cross the stile into the second field on the right. Follow the path
to the right of a small modern housing development and turn
right down a lane under the substantial bridge of a disused railway line. Bear right over the main road to cross the road-bridge
over the River Wye at Glasbury.

There are few opportunities to cross the River Wye and indeed
there is no other crossing between Glasbury and Hay-on-Wye. The
old village is south of the road on the west side of the river and a
detour is therefore necessary to see old houses dating back as far as

N.B. NORTH IS NOT AT THE TOP OF THIS MAP!

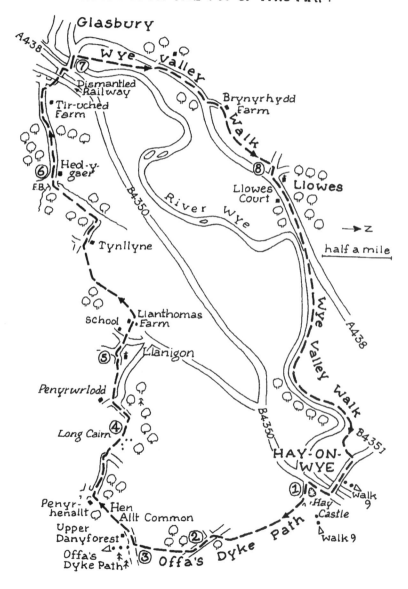

1400. Little remains of the medieval church having been destroyed as the river changed course.

7. Immediately after passing over the bridge turn right to cross a stile, joining the Wye Valley Walk. Walk alongside the fence to the right through a succession of kissing gates and then bear left to pass a finger post. Cross a track and 50 metres later turn right along a road for a generous quarter of a mile. At the end of a sweeping right-hand bend turn left up a surfaced track, pass through a farm then bear right on a path to contour along the hillside, where there are some lovely views over the river. Shortly after, at a junction of paths, bear right as waymarked to continue contouring through woodland and cross a stile to descend towards a terrace of cottages. Turn right down the lane into the village of Llowes.

St Meilig's Church was rebuilt in the 1850s and is frequently mentioned in Kilvert's diaries. Francis Kilvert was a Victorian cleric who, whilst living in the neighbouring village of Clyro, kept a diary giving a valuable insight into life at that time in the border country. St Meilig's was the church of his friend, Tom Williams. Inside the church is a scheduled ancient monument – St Meilig's Cross – weighing some three and a half tons. It is a Celtic type wheel-cross and one of the most impressive early Christian crosses to be seen in this country.

8. Turn left to pass through the churchyard and then turn left along the road again for about a quarter of a mile. After passing through a lay-by, bear right along a path and cross a stile on the right to reach the riverbank. The path now follows the riverbank for some one and a half miles. Turn left along a track by a cottage leaving the river and then turn right over a waymarked footbridge. Bear right up a clear path through woodland and bear left to cross a stile where Hay-on-Wye comes into view. Go along the top edge of a field and turn right down the road into the town. The shortest route back to the car park is to turn right along Broad Street, and follow signs to the information centre.

Walk 11: Craswall Priory from below Hay Bluff

Starting point: Grid reference 239373, car park at the intersection of lanes under Hay Bluff

Distance: 8 miles (12.9 kilometres)

Height gain: 1000 feet (300 metres)

Maps: Outdoor Leisure 13 (Brecon Beacons National Park – East), Landranger 161 (Abergavenny and Black Mountains)

Facilities: Full facilities in Hay-on-Wye

Terrain: An initially gentle walk across open moorland before descending to pass the remains of the old priory. The walk then continues undulating through fields and woodland before the final climb back to the car park. Some soft ground is likely to be encountered in the second half of the walk.

The countryside here is dominated by Hay Bluff rising to over 2200 feet above sea level where weather conditions can be severe. At such times, this walk is a useful alternative to number 12.

1. Walk down the lane towards Hay-on-Wye for about 300 metres and then turn right by a marker post joining the Offa's Dyke Trail. Follow this clear track towards Hay Bluff for about 300 metres, ford a shallow stream and bear left, leaving the Offa's Dyke Trail until the last section of the walk. Ignore a left turn downhill and contour along the hillside. Subsequently, a fence climbing from the left and then a stone wall joins the path. Pass through a field gate, the path having evolved to a track, to continue alongside a wire fence.

2. Pass through another gate and bear right, diverging slowly from the obvious track. Carry on through a waymarked handgate in the fence ahead and along a faint grassy track to go through another handgate and continue down the centre of the ridge. Bear left of the fence ahead to descend alongside it to a handgate. Turn left along a lane and then right down the waymarked bridleway, signposted to Abbey Farm approximately half a mile away in the valley.

Descending into the valley note the ruins of Craswall Priory away to the right – sadly, little remains other than a few walls. This small priory was one of only three houses of the Grandmontine Order founded in this country and dates from the early 13th century.

Wild ponies under Hay Bluff

3. Bear right through the waymarked gate alongside the cattle-grid and rejoin the track winding uphill and into the farmyard. Facing the farmhouse turn right to pass through a waymarked gate, beside the barn at the top end of the farmyard, and climb up a track to a junction of paths as evidenced by waymarkers on the gatepost ahead. Turn left to contour across a field above the farm and join a clear track. Where this path peters out, follow overhead wires then pass through a field gate and bear left to pass through another gate. Follow the overhead wires again to the second pole and then turn left to contour across the field to a lane.

4. Turn right down the lane and, after going round a sweeping left-hand bend, cross the stile on the right by a prominent finger

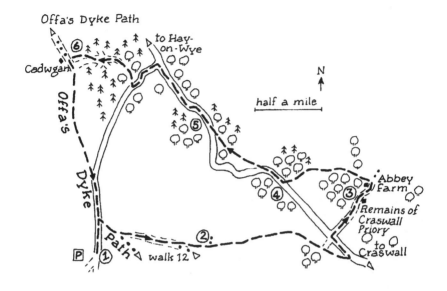

post. Go down the field towards the bottom pole carrying over-head wires and then bear right to circumvent a gully. Turn left between hawthorn trees to cross the stile/footbridge combination over a stream. Bear right over the next field and, where the ground is terraced down to the woodland, pass between isolated hawthorn trees to find a marker post in the edge of the woods. Descend through the woods increasingly steeply as directed, where the path is not obvious, to the footbridge over a stream. On the other side of the bridge, climb up into a clearing, which is part of a long narrow field between the woods and a lane. Contour along this field to cross a stile, hidden in the hedge to the left, roughly halfway between two gates.

5. Turn right down the lane for about a half-mile to a junction and turn left up the lane signposted to Capel-y-ffin. Turn right at the end of the fence on the right-hand side and bear left by a waymarker to ford a stream. Turn right to pass through the handgate along a clear path at the edge of woodland. Continue along the top edge of a field and then bear left to follow the clear bridleway into the woods by way of a handgate.

6. Bear right across a forest track and after passing through the next handgate turn left up an enclosed path, rejoining the Offa's Dyke Trail. Bear right up the open pasture parallel to the fence on the right until the road comes into view. Converge progressively with the road to return to the car park.

Walk 12: Hay Bluff and around Black Hill

Starting point: Grid reference 239373, car park at the base of Hay Bluff

Distance: 12 miles (19.3 kilometres)

Height gain: 1700 feet (520 metres)

Maps: Outdoor Leisure 13 (Brecon Beacons National Park – East), Landranger 161 (Abergavenny and Black Mountains)

Facilities: Full facilities in Hay-on-Wye. Public house at Craswall, a short detour from the route of the walk

Terrain: Straightforward route finding after locating the path which climbs up to the ridge and the ground is generally firm. The path follows the official trail route up to the ridge, rather than the "black dot" path, past the trig point that is also promoted in the national trail guide. The latter more direct and steep route is not, however, a right of way. Use of this route is also creating an unsightly scar on the hillside.

Hay Bluff rises steeply about 600 feet above the car park to some 2200 feet above sea level. The weather at this very exposed point on the edge of the Brecon Beacons is potentially the most severe to be encountered on these walks. Consider the weather forecast and wear or carry appropriate protective clothing. If you can't see the top of the bluff is there any point in risking an accident by undertaking the walk on this particular day?

1. Walk down the road from the car park and turn right by a marker post to join the Offa's Dyke Trail. Follow waymarkers at junctions, which will generally direct walkers along the higher path, to climb obliquely up the side of Hay Bluff. Bear right as waymarked nearing the ridge to reach a junction of paths, where the unofficial trail goes right and over the top of Hay Bluff.

This junction is near a rocky outcrop known as Llech y Lladron (translation – Robber's Stone) just below another short climb to cross the 700 metre contour which is slightly higher than the trig point at the end of Hay Bluff.

Golden Valley from Hay Bluff

2. Turn left up the ridge to the high point about a half-mile further on. Continue on the well-worn path along the ridge, following a line of cairns over barren ground where the path is indistinct. On reaching a tombstone indicating a cross-path, turn left along the path signposted to Olchon Valley.

> *On the other side of the valley is Black Hill from which a narrow ridge, called Cat's Back Ridge, runs south-easterly descending progressively to the valley. This walk bends around the back of Cat's Back Ridge and Black Hill although there is also a "black dot" path along this ridge from the picnic site which is passed at reference point 4.*

3. After a few hundred metres the path bends left to descend obliquely down the side of the ridge. Nearing the bottom of the hill follow the path bending right to a marker post, then turn left straight down the lower slope and through two gates to a lane. Turn right past Olchon Court and a cottage before turning left down a well-waymarked diverted path beside a stream. Cross Olchon Brook and bear right to pass to the right of a farm and

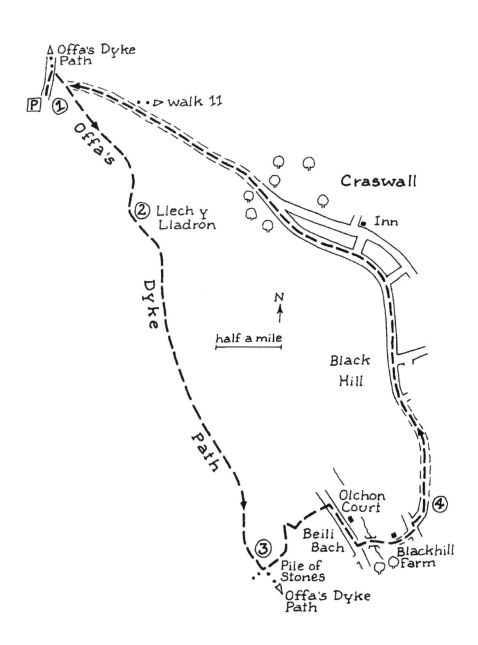

alongside a stream climbing steeply through woodland to another lane. Turn left along this lane and right at the next junction to a small picnic site with good views, which is a very suitable place for lunch.

4. Cross the stile at the end of the lane to continue along a waymarked track, which contours along the side of Black Hill for some two miles (ignoring right turns). The bridleway then narrows and continues along the top side of fields, by way of handgates. At a cross-track, immediately after passing through another handgate, turn right to soon reach a surfaced lane. Turn left along this lane which soon deteriorates to a rough track. This track climbs progressively to the open heathland under Hay Bluff and initially follows the boundary fence to the right. At the far end of this fence, now bordering a conifer plantation, contour around the hillside to emerge on the road below the car park.

Walk 13: Hatterrall Ridge from Longtown

Starting point: Grid reference 323288, car park adjacent to the village hall approximately 200 metres up the road from the post office

Distance: 7 miles (11.3 kilometres)

Height gain: 1250 feet (380 metres)

Maps: Outdoor Leisure 13 (Brecon Beacons National Park – East), Landranger 161 (Abergavenny and Black Mountains)

Facilities: Full facilities in Hay-on-Wye, public houses in Longtown and Clodock

Terrain: Straightforward path and gradual climb up to the ridge. Equally gradual descent and firm field paths back to Longtown.

Turn left out of the car park and walk up the lane to see Longtown Castle dating from the 12th century and remarkable for the cylindrical keep which is the most significant feature to have survived.

1. Return to the lane on the right before reaching the car park and go down this lane. Turn left over a stile just before the lane crosses Olchon Brook to walk parallel to the brook. After 60 metres turn right over the footbridge and then cross the stile ahead to bear left along a farm track, starting the climb to the ridge.

2. Follow this track through the farm and continue up two fields by the hedge to the right. Cross a stile and then progressively diverge from the hedge to cross another stile in the top fence and join an enclosed track. Climb over a stile and go through the adjacent handgate before proceeding straight uphill to the corner of the fence to the left. Bear left to climb obliquely along a clear path briefly joined by a fence to the left. Approaching the top of the ridge, fork right to intersect the Offa's Dyke Trail. Turn left along the trail and continue for about two miles.

3. Pass a tombstone indicating the path down to Cwmyoy and, at the next tombstone signposted to Oldcastle, turn left and leave the Offa's Dyke Trail. After 20 metres bear left at a marker post and contour back along the hillside to a finger post. Bear right to descend obliquely along a clear path to a wire fence by a ruined farm and bear left alongside the fence. After a half-mile, this path develops into a track between mature hedges, still contouring along the side of the valley for a further third of a mile.

"Tombstone" indicating the path down to Oldcastle

4. Pass through a gate into a small clearing to climb the stile adjacent to the middle gate and walk on for about 50 metres. Bear right diagonally down a field, cross a stile/bridge combination, and descend alongside a hedge to join a stony track at the bottom of the field. Pass through a farmyard where the surface improves. Continue down a lane to a T-junction and cross the stile opposite to bear left across a field. Cross a stile/bridge combination, a farm track and another stile. Cross the next field diagonally and a further stile/bridge to walk towards the tower of the church in the hamlet of Clodock.

> *Sant Clydawg (Clodock!) has a nave and chancel arch dating from Norman times – the arch is notably large for that age. The tower is 15th century and there are 17th-century furnishings. The nearby Cornewall Arms is a very old-fashioned village pub where opening hours, during the daytime at least, are erratic.*

5. Pass through the churchyard to the diagonally opposite corner. Bear left alongside the River Monnow, then, in the second field, diverge from the river and pass through a gate. Go through the next field, with a hedge to the right, and then carry on in the

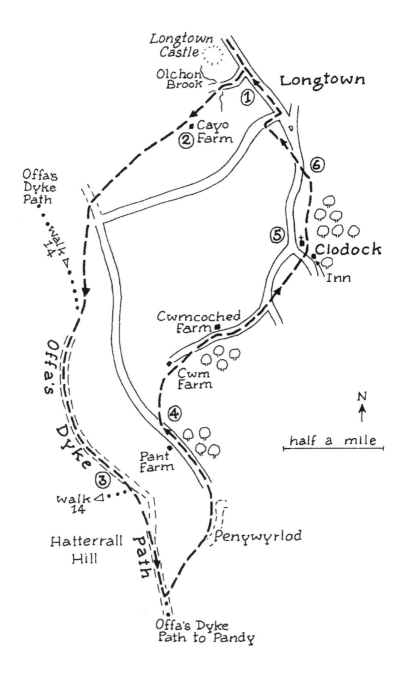

Longtown
Castle
Olchon
Brook
Longtown
①
② Cayo Farm
⑥
Offa's
Dyke
Path
walk 14 ▷
Clodock
⑤
Inn
Offa's Dyke Path
Cwmcoched
Farm
N
↑
half a mile
Cwm
Farm
④
Pant
Farm
③
walk ◁
14
Hatterrall
Hill
Penywyrlod
Offa's Dyke
Path to Pandy

same direction to cross a stone stile. Turn left to cross two more stone stiles and turn right along the lane towards Longtown.

6. Cross a bridge and immediately turn left over another stone stile. Walk past the left-hand corner of the wooden fence ahead, crossing the stile on the right, to continue in the same direction until reaching a lane. Turn right to emerge on the main road through the village and turn left past the post office.

Walk 14: Hatterrall Hill and Cwmyoy from Llanthony Priory

Starting point: Grid reference 288278, car park by Llanthony Priory which is inclined to fill up early at peak holiday times

Distance: 10.5 miles (16.9 kilometres)

Height gain: 1400 feet (430 metres)

Maps: Outdoor Leisure 13 (Brecon Beacons National Park - East), Landranger 161 (Abergavenny and Black Mountains)

Facilities: Refreshment and toilet facilities in Llanthony, full facilities in Hay-on-Wye or Abergavenny.

Terrain: This walk starts with a severe climb to the ridge, during which the path is quite clear. After following the trail along the ridge, the path down to Cwmyoy is initially faint but there are no side paths to cause confusion except in the valley near Cwmyoy. The last part of the walk along the valley is generally straightforward. After the first half-mile, which can be very muddy, most of the walk is along firm tracks.

Llanthony has become a very popular starting point for walks and the priory is a highly recommended detour from the Offa's Dyke Trail, which passes along the ridge above. Llanthony Priory has a long and interesting history. From 1103 and, even before this date, there was a chapel on the site dedicated to St David. The present buildings are largely late-12th and early-13th century but the priory was already in decline before the Reformation. The owner, in the 18th century, converted the south tower into a shooting box and the canon's quarters into a house for his steward. The latter is now the hotel overlooking the cloisters. The ruins still demonstrate the transition from the Norman (round arches) to the Gothic (pointed arches) in the building of the priory in a hauntingly beautiful setting.

1. Walk out of the car park, between the priory and the church, to cross the stile ahead and turn right up the track signposted "circular walk Hatterrall Hill". Continue uphill following the finger post bearing the legend "Offa's Dyke North" and turn left by a marker post to cross a stile. Bear right up the first field to cross the stile clearly in view and continue in the same direction up the next field to cross two stiles in quick succession, passing very briefly through woodland. Carry on uphill past a marker post to go through a handgate onto the unfenced hillside.

2. Bear left up the steep well-worn path and pass old quarry workings, where the path becomes a permitted route rather than right of way. At a small cluster of trees the path bends right where the gradient also becomes less severe. Attaining the ridge, pass a small cairn and bear right to the next cairn, already in view, which marks the junction with the Offa's Dyke Trail. At this point, where there is also a tombstone, turn right onto a fabulous ridge walk for about three miles.

3. Follow the trail past a trig point and cross-path to Longtown and Llanthony as indicated by a tombstone. After a short climb turn right by a cairn and tombstone signposted to Cwmyoy, leaving the Offa's Dyke Trail, and proceed along the narrow but distinct path along the top of Hatterrall Hill. Bear left at a fork in the path by a small cairn to start the increasingly steep descent towards Cwmyoy. At the foot of the hill turn left and soon pass through a gate before turning right down a track. At a fork in the track by a National Park notice board, bear left down a sunken path to a lane and turn left. Turn right into the churchyard to visit a distinctively shaped church.

> *The church of St Martin is certainly an arresting sight with the tower leaning at a crazy angle accentuated by the chancel leaning in the opposite direction! Closer inspection reveals that huge buttresses support the whole structure. This building dates back at least to the Middle Ages and has suffered subsidence at various times but nonetheless survived to this time. There is a medieval cross inside the church.*

4. Turn left by the cross in the churchyard and turn right down a lane to the road junction. Turn right past the telephone box and, before crossing the river turn right along a track passing through fields. After this track peters out bear right to cross a stile by a gate in the middle of the hedge and continue in the same direction along the bottom edge of fields. Cross two stiles descending to a track and turn right to the main road along the valley.

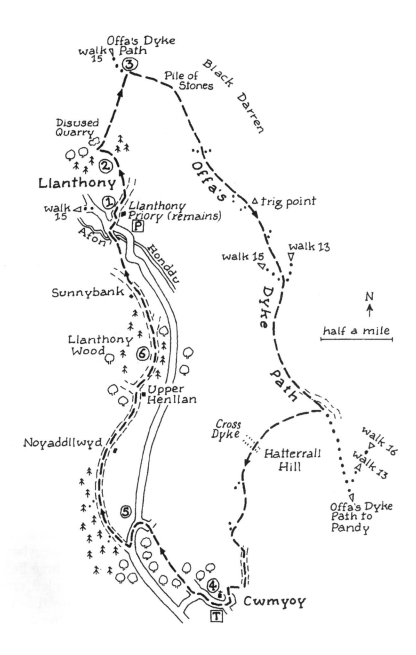

Offa's Dyke
walk Path
15
③
Pile of
Stones
Black Darren
Disused
Quarry
②
Llanthony
walk ◁
15
①
Llanthony
Priory (remains)
P
Afon
Honddu
Offa's
△ trig point
walk 15
△
walk 13
▽
Sunnybank
Dyke
N
↑
half a mile
Llanthony
Wood
⑥
Path
Upper
Henllan
Cross
Dyke
walk 16
▽
Noyaddllwyd
Hatterrall
Hill
walk 13
△
▽
Offa's Dyke
Path to
Pandy
⑤
④
i
Cwmyoy
T

Cwmyoy church: the tower and chancel lean in opposite directions

5. Turn left along the road for over 300 metres and then turn right up an enclosed waymarked track. Pass around the top side of a house and contour along a path through woodland. Bear left to pass above a farm briefly joining a stony track before bearing right, just before a cattle-grid, to go through a gate and pass around the bottom edge of another stretch of woodland. Leave these woods behind and bear left past another farm. Bear right at the next junction of tracks passing through a gate and fording a small stream. Continue contouring along the hillside beside a fence to the right and join a clearer track before entering Llanthony Wood.

6. At the point where this track starts to descend bear left along a fairly level path to pass a cottage and join another track. At a hairpin bend go straight on along a track and pass Sunnybank. Turn right over a stile and walk diagonally down three fields crossing numerous stiles. After fording a stream, bear left, cross another stile and a footbridge over the river to follow the clear track into Llanthony. Bear left across the main road to return to the car park.

Walk 15: The Vale of Ewyas and Hatterrall Ridge from Llanthony Priory

Starting point: Grid reference 288278, car park adjacent to Llanthony Priory (which fills up early at peak holiday times)

Distance: 10.5 miles (16.9 kilometres)

Height gain: 1500 feet (460 metres)

Maps: Outdoor Leisure 13 (Brecon Beacons National Park – East), Landranger 161 (Abergavenny and Black Mountains)

Facilities: Refreshments and toilets in Llanthony, full facilities in Hay-on-Wye or Abergavenny

Terrain: Mainly open ground firstly up one side and then traversing the valley to climb up to the ridge. Firm tracks and paths predominate and there is one steep ascent. Streams to be encountered in the first two miles may be difficult to ford if they are swollen by heavy rain. The first half of this walk is relatively energetic and slow before a walk along the ridge for 4 miles and an easy descent. Route-finding is not always straightforward before joining the Offa's Dyke Trail.

Nowadays Llanthony is a focal point for walkers but historically it has also been an important religious site. Its name is a corruption of the Welsh, meaning 'Church of St David by the Honddu Brook'. The Augustinian Priory was established early in the 12th century but the present buildings date from the turn of the century. The present church, also 13th century, was probably created out of the priory infirmary and chapel.

1. Walk out of the car park, cross the stile opposite and bear left down a field along the path signposted to Capel-y-ffin. Cross a stile to go along the lane, which runs the full length of the valley, pass the pub and bear left at a fork to stay on the major road for another 300 metres. Turn left up the waymarked enclosed sunken path (which is always muddy because of a spring about 100 metres up the path), pass through two handgates and turn right.

Llanthony Priory against the background of Hatterrall Ridge

2. Initially the path contours outside the fencing at the top end of the field system and then bears left uphill. Where this clear path bends sharply left, walk straight on along the less obvious grassy path descending to a finger post. Ford a stream running past the farm below and then cross a stile, where a waymarker indicates that walkers are now on a permitted path continuing for about 600 metres. Ascend obliquely along a grassy track that levels off after crossing the next stile.

3. Pass above a farm and soon after ford another stream before forking right down a bridleway. Pass through a field gate and a handgate before proceeding along the bottom edge of fields (a permitted path about 100 metres long passes above Sychtre Farm at a slightly higher level than the right of way). Climb a stile to walk briefly on the other side of the hedge then revert to having the hedge to the right.

4. At a cluster of three stiles by a barn, cross one stile only to carry on along the bottom edge of fields and then cross a stile in the bottom hedge, just before reaching a gate ahead, to continue in

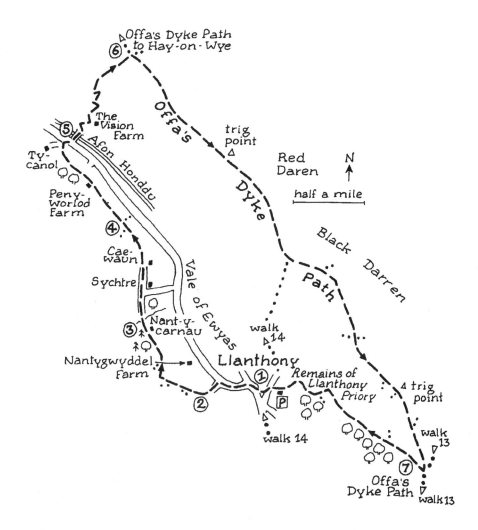

the same direction. After climbing another stile turn left by a marker post into the adjacent farmyard, and immediately turn right along a track. Fork left along the top side of the field and pass through a gate to continue along the bottom edge of fields. In the second field, adjacent to a ruined building, cross the stile on the right to walk along the top edge of the field and then turn right down to the lane.

A little way further up the lane, and probably best visited by car in view of the volume of traffic using this winding road, is Capel-y-ffin (Chapel on the boundary) which has three ecclesiastical buildings. There are two chapels in the hamlet and, a quarter of a mile to the west, Llanthony monastery which was started in 1870 by the Reverend J.L. Lyne, who had been frustrated in his attempts to acquire and restore the priory. The monastery fell into disrepair after the death of Lyne, then known as Father Ignatius, in 1908.

5. Cross the stile on the opposite side of the lane and bear right to cross the footbridge over a stream. Bear left to climb up two fields to cross a stile under a large tree. Turn left along a farm track and bear right over a stile signposted "To the hill" and "Offa's Dyke". Bear right uphill and turn sharp right on passing a marker post. Turn left at the next marker post to climb directly uphill and cross two stiles. Turn right to contour along the hillside and after 80 metres bear left (as waymarked on a gatepost) to follow a clear path, winding back and forth up the hill. At a junction of paths by a tombstone bear right to climb more gradually to the ridge, in the process bending right past a marker stone where the path is less clear.

6. A cairn and a tombstone mark the junction of this path with the Offa's Dyke Trail. Turn right along the very well-worn path along the ridge, passing two trig points and tombstones indicating side paths to Red Daren and Llanthony. This is a glorious ridge walk with the contrasting views of the Brecons to the right and the flat rich farming country of Herefordshire to the left.

7. About a half-mile after the second trig point, on reaching another tombstone indicating a cross-path to Longtown and Llanthony, turn sharply right commencing the gradual descent to Llanthony. The path is obvious until nearing the valley floor. At a junction of paths, turn left over a stile and walk directly downhill towards woodland. Climb another stile and bear right down a clear path through the woods. Emerging from the woodland, the right of way passes diagonally down the field towards the priory. The waymark on the stile, however, directs walkers along the top and then down the side of the field, which I am told is the farmer's preference. Cross the stile at the bottom of the field to bear right alongside the boundary wall of the priory and turn left down a track to the stile crossed at the beginning of the walk.

Walk 16: Walterstone and Hatterrall Hill

Starting point: Grid reference 331221, lane off A465 Hereford – Abergavenny road near Pandy. Follow the side road past the Pandy Inn and, at the next bend, turn left past Trewyn Lodge to park on the broad grass verge beyond Brynhonddu Lodge.

Distance: 8.5 miles (13.7 kilometres)

Height gain: 1600 feet (490 metres)

Maps: Outdoor Leisure 13 (Brecon Beacons National Park – East), Landranger 161 (Abergavenny and Black Mountains)

Facilities: Full facilities in Abergavenny, inns in Walterstone and Pandy, hotel near the start of the walk

Terrain: Quiet country lanes and tracks plus an energetic climb to the ridge and a gradual descent. There is a short boggy stretch around the earthworks of the hill fort otherwise firm ground.

There is, unfortunately, no convenient car park or lay-by for this walk but use of the broad grass verge well away from gateways and bends will leave the lane clear for other traffic.

1. Walk back down the lane to the junction by Trewyn Lodge and climb the stile opposite to cross a field towards the farm in view ahead. Cross a stile in the corner of the field and turn right along the lane past the farm. Pass the hotel and turn right up a lane signposted to Walterstone Common. After ascending gradually for a good mile, and just before reaching a white house opposite to a farm, turn left over a waymarked stile. Walk alongside the fence bounding woodland – the site of an ancient hill fort.

   This large and complex fortification dates back to the Iron Age, the main concentric embankments are complicated by other earthworks indicating a site of some significance. There are also remains of a motte and bailey behind the cottages opposite Walterstone church whilst a Roman mosaic is said to been found locally which all suggests the area has been settled over a long period.

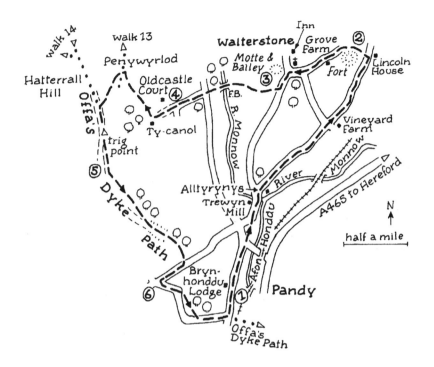

2. Carry on alongside the fence bearing left over the earthworks and descend to cross a stile. Follow the sunken lane downhill; pass through a farm to go forward down a track. Pass Rockyfold, where the owners have landscaped the area around a waterfall on the right, and walk straight on along a lane to Walterstone.

St Mary's Church, the pub and cottages are nicely huddled together in this hamlet. Whilst these buildings are not particularly old or architecturally significant they do form a very harmonious grouping.

3. Turn left at the T-junction and 50 metres after passing Road Cottage turn right over a stile, cross the first field converging with the fence on the right, and in the next field carry on alongside a stream. Climb the stile by a gate, bear left then right to cross the substantial footbridge over the River Monnow. Turn right up-

Footbridge over the Monnow

stream briefly and then follow the hedge to the left towards the ridge. Go over a stile in the top left-hand corner of the field and bear left across a lane to follow a track towards Oldcastle Court.

4. Climb increasingly steeply past the old church, now deconsecrated, and go through the farmyard of Oldcastle Court to follow the concrete track to the next farm. Turn right up an enclosed track (ignoring the gully from which a stream emerges) and continue along the bottom of a large field. Passing a metal gate, bear left diagonally up the field towards the far-top corner, as indicated by the waymarker on the gatepost. Continue in the same direction over stiles to a ruined farmstead and turn left through the waymarked gate onto the open hillside. Turn right alongside the fence for 50 metres and then turn sharply left to climb obliquely up to the ridge on a clear path. Bear left at a finger post near the top to intersect the Offa's Dyke Trail by a tombstone. Turn left along the trail and, after a quarter-mile, bear left to pass a trig point and start the (generally) gradual descent.

There are glorious views both over Golden Valley to the left and the contrasting Brecons on the right.

5. After a further 250 metres, just before two tracks merge, bear left down a less obvious path which soon passes to the left of a large walled enclosure, before converging briefly with a track and another stone wall. Follow the grassy path, as indicated by the finger post, now diverging from the track to pass to the right of a small enclosure of conifers and follow the stone wall steeply downhill. Cross a stile and carry on down an enclosed sunken lane, at the end of which turn right along a lane to crossroads.

6. Turn left past a very small chapel and, just beyond a converted barn, bear left over a stile to descend progressively across a large field to the bottom corner. Go over the stile and turn left down a lane. Turn left at the T-junction, leaving the Offa's Dyke Trail, to return to your vehicle.

Walk 17: The Skirrid from Llanvihangel Crucorney

Starting point: Grid reference 326207, car park adjacent to the general store in the village off the A465 (note: charge payable)

Distance: 9.5 miles (15.3 kilometres)

Height gain: 1800 feet (550 metres)

Maps: Outdoor Leisure 13 (Brecon Beacons National Park – East), Landranger 161 (Abergavenny and Black Mountains)

Facilities: Full facilities in Abergavenny, public houses in Llanvihangel Crucorney and Llangattock Lingoed

Terrain: A lengthy, increasingly steep, climb to the top of the Skirrid (Ysgyryd Fawr) followed by field paths over undulating ground creating a fairly strenuous walk.

The village is pleasantly quiet following the construction of the by-pass and is dominated by the Skirrid Inn said to date from 1100 and to be the oldest inn in Wales. Llanvihangel Court, on the other side of the by-pass, is a lovely Elizabethan manor house (open to the public). Pen-y-Clawdd, one mile away to the south-west, is a superb late medieval manor house with a motte and bailey castle nearby (also open to the public).

1. Turn right out of the car park and walk through the village past the Skirrid Inn and the church. Cross the main road towards the bus stop and go through the gap in the hedge nearby to walk along the old A465. Where the old road bends right by Orchard House go straight on along a track, waymarked Llwyn Franc, through a succession of gates and past a barn (where a permitted path has been established utilising this track as a more straight-forward alternative to the right of way). Follow the track sharply left uphill and, at the top of the second field on the right, turn right along the top of two fields to turn left up a lane for about a half-mile.

2. 20 metres before a sharp right-hand bend turn right over a stile, signposted to Skirrid Fawr, hidden in a hedge between two gates. Walk uphill to the left of ruined farm buildings and cross

two stiles in quick succession to bear right to another stile already in view. Turn right up the side of two fields and pass through a handgate to the open ground at the foot of the Skirrid.

3. Turn left along the path which circles the base of the Skirrid, until abreast of a stile in the fence to the left, then turn right up the well-worn grassy path. Walk initially straight uphill, and then briefly bear right before turning sharply left to climb obliquely to the ridge. Turn right along the ridge to the trig point where there are spectacular panoramic views in particular north and west to the Brecons, with the renowned Blorenge (1832 ft) and Sugar Loaf (1955ft) in the foreground.

Looking towards the Brecons from the top of The Skirrid

The Skirrid, 1601 feet above sea level and now National Trust land, is regarded as a Holy Mountain, the fissure on the west side allegedly being caused by a landslip at the time of the Crucifixion. An Iron Age hill fort was established on the top and there was a Roman Catholic Chapel (St Michael's) used in the 17th century to escape religious persecution. Nothing remains of the chapel other than the two upright stones near the trig point.

4. Return to the base of the hill by the same route and cross the last-mentioned stile. Proceed towards the gates in the bottom

corner of the field and turn left over the stile by the water-trough to walk alongside the fence to the right. Where this fence bends right, climb the stile to go down the middle of a large triangular field as waymarked. In the bottom corner turn sharp left to climb alongside the fence for about 75 metres and turn right over a stile to go along the bottom of the next field. In the bottom corner of this field cross the stile on the right and continue in the same direction to a lane.

5. Walk down the lane to a T-junction, cross the stile opposite and go forward through the gate in the hedge ahead. Pass along the right side of a field and, just before reaching a farm, turn right to a concreted track then turn left along the track into the farm complex. Where the concrete finishes go through the double and single gates ahead and turn right. Bear left down the field to pass through a gate and forward in the same direction over a stile down to a stream in the valley.

6. Cross a footbridge to continue in roughly the same direction diagonally up a field to cross a stile about 20 metres higher than a gateway. Bear left up the next field to pass through the right-hand of three gates in the hedge ahead and cross a narrow field and stile. Go down into another valley, walking alongside a fence, and continue in the same direction in the next field. Bear left by a telegraph pole to cross a complex of stiles, a ford and a bridge at the confluence of two streams. Pass in front of a cottage to cross another stile and walk up a field, diagonally towards the top corner. Turn left over a stile, joining the Offa's Dyke Trail, to pass through the churchyard of the parish church of Llangattock Lingoed.

St Cadoc's Church, in a very picturesque setting, dates from the 13th century, as does the nearby Hunter's Moon Inn.

7. Turn left along the lane (or right to detour to the inn!) and bear right up steps to follow an enclosed path. Continue along the bottom of fields before crossing a stile to carry on alongside the same hedge and then bear left downhill to a stream. Cross a footbridge to carry on in roughly the same direction steeply uphill and then, in the next field, contour along the hillside. Passing a cottage under renovation bear left down to a stile to walk along-

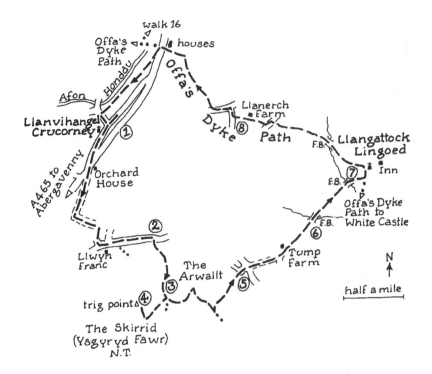

side a stream to a lane. Turn left for 100 metres then turn right over a waymarked stile and climb up a field, to pass to the left of a farm, to join the farm track to another lane.

8. Turn right and, at a T-junction, turn left for 100 metres, then turn right to cross a field towards the right side of a small copse. Cross a stile/bridge combination to contour across the next field and again descend to the right of woodland. Contour across the next field, follow the top edge of another field, and subsequently go forward to cross the left-hand of two stiles. Walk down to the main road, turn left along the road, leaving the Offa's Dyke Trail, before bearing right over a stile signposted to Pen-y-bont. Cross the broad bridge over a ditch and a large field to a stile on the left side of a ruined barn. Go along the back of a campsite and the bottom edge of a field before turning left up a lane to the centre of Llanvihangel Crucorney.

Walk 18: White Castle and Llantilio Crossenny from Llanvetherine

Starting point: Grid reference 364173, lay-by on B4521 opposite Llanvetherine church

Distance: 7 miles (11.3 kilometres)

Height gain: 650 feet (200 metres)

Maps: Outdoor Leisure 13 (Brecon Beacons National Park – East), Landranger 161 (Abergavenny and Black Mountains)

Facilities: Full facilities in Abergavenny, public houses in Llanvetherine and Llantilio Crossenny

Terrain: A mixture of field paths, tracks and country lanes involving two gradual climbs up to White Castle

---

The feature of the church of St James which should be immediately apparent is the unusual castellated tower. The church probably dates from the 14th century and the most noteworthy features inside are carved stones around the altar, including one very old stone believed to depict a saint and 17th-century memorials to a priest and his wife. The village was on an old drove road between Ross-on-Wye and Abergavenny.

1. Cross the stile in the adjacent hedge and bear right to go up to the corner of the field. Climb a stile behind the large tree to contour across the next two fields and then join a lane to descend to the road. Turn left along the road, passing a chapel and finger posts for the Offa's Dyke Trail and the Three Castles Way, which also uses this stretch of road.

2. Turn right over a stile, 100 metres after passing the left turn to Bont, and join the Three Castles Way. Pass to the left of the trees and a ditch to cross a field and a footbridge before bearing right to climb a stile. Turn left to proceed up the side of fields, crossing numerous stiles, and then bear left of the woodland ahead to cross another stile. Follow an enclosed path along the side of the woodland to White Castle.

The impressive ruins of White Castle

This castle together with those at Grosmont and Skenfrith formed an important strategic triangular defence against the Welsh. White Castle, one of the best-preserved fortresses of the Marches, is the largest and oldest of the three having been developed in the 12th and 13th centuries. It is likely that the name was acquired by reference to a white plaster covering of the stone, a little of which can still be seen. Alternatively, it could have been named after a Welsh chief called Gwyn (translation – white), but the castle's purpose makes this a remote possibility!

3. Continue down the lane by the castle for about a quarter of a mile and, 100 metres after passing Pear Tree Barn, turn left over a stile. Go forward across further stiles and the intervening small paddocks into the valley. Cross the footbridge over a stream and walk on past a marker post to cross another footbridge. Climb up the next field alongside a hedge to the right following marker posts. Continue in the same direction contouring across two fields, whilst enjoying sweeping views to the south, and then cross a stile to turn right over a ditch. Climb up the right side of the next field and, approaching a lane, cross two adjacent stiles to turn right down this quiet lane past Middle Cwm Farm.

There should be a public footpath on the right, immediately after passing this farm, to the B4233 by the entrance to Park Farm. When it has been reinstated, use of this path avoids, in particular, walking along the B4233. Briefly,this path, descends to pass to the left of a copse before bearing right to the road; it is not intersected by any other footpath. It should therefore be followed without difficulty when the appropriate stiles and waymarking are in place.

4. Carry on down the lane for a generous half-mile leaving the Three Castles Way and turn right along the B4233. Go through the waymarked handgate, opposite to the entrance of Park Farm, to cross a field towards the right-hand end of a stone wall and then follow this wall to the village church of Llantilio Crossenny.

This is the nearest settlement to White Castle and the name means the Church of St Teilo at Iddon's Cross. Iddon was a local chieftain who enlisted the help of a holy man, Teilo, to help him defeat the Saxons. Iddon then rewarded Teilo with the land on which the first church was built in the 6th century. The present church, dating from the 13th and 14th centuries, is on a mound just as the earlier timber church would have been sited. There is also a moated rectangular enclosure bordering the lane leading in the direction of White Castle, on which there once was a medieval dwelling (Old Court).

5. Turn right down the lane by the church and, 50 metres before reaching the 15th-century Hostry Inn, turn right through a kissing gate joining the Offa's Dyke Trail. Go forward across two fields, a lane and another field bearing left of a large isolated oak tree. Climb a stile and veer left to cross a ditch, then climb up the next two fields to cross another stile by a copse. Now descend gradually alongside the hedge to the right, where there is an excellent view of the Skirrid, and then bear left of the farm ahead. Turn left down the farm track, turn right along a lane for about 150 metres and then turn right up a roughly surfaced lane. Fol-

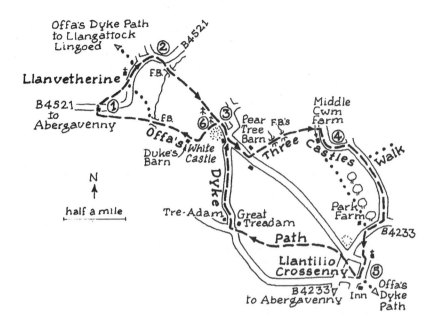

low this lane for a generous half-mile and then continue up the lane ahead to again pass White Castle.

6. Bear left along an enclosed path bending around the outer wall of the castle to cross a stile and bear right down the side of a large field. 20 metres from the bottom corner turn right over a stile to pass alongside barns, and after 75 metres, climb a stile in the adjacent hedge to continue in the same direction. Cross the stile ahead and turn left down the edge of a field to bear right on reaching the second field gate. Climb the stile in the bottom hedge, to cross the valley by way of a footbridge, and go on to a marker post denoting a junction of paths at the corner of a hedge. Bear left across the field, leaving the Offa's Dyke Trail, to cross another footbridge and bear right along the edge of two fields. Cross a stile and turn right up the enclosed path to the churchyard.

Walk 19: King's Wood and Treowen from Dingestow

Starting point: Grid reference 457104, lay-by at the side of the church which is about 200 metres outside the village of Dingestow, but the tower is visible from the village centre

Distance: 5 miles (8 kilometres)

Height gain: 650 feet (200 metres)

Maps: Outdoor Leisure 14 (Wye Valley and Forest of Dean), Landranger 161 (Abergavenny and Black Mountains)

Facilities: Full facilities in Monmouth, pubs about half a mile outside Dingestow and in Mitchel Troy

Terrain: Mostly firm tracks linked by field paths and a quiet country lane on this gentle climb to a wooded hill. This is the shortest walk in the book and can be completed easily in a half-day or summer evening.

St Dingat's Church, extensively restored in the 19th century but nonetheless attractive in the Early English style, is named after the Celtic saint who founded the church here. The nearby castle, of Norman origin, was demolished in the 19th century – supposedly for use as roadstone.

1. Walk down the lane away from the village, soon passing the site of the castle, where all that remains is a mound. On reaching a finger post turn right over the adjacent stile, cross the nearby bridge over a ditch and continue in the same direction over a footbridge and a field with the River Trothy to the right. Go along the bottom of the next field before bearing left to climb the stile and then veer right to cross another stile by a gate. Bear right around the corner of the hedge ahead and then cross a stile in the middle of the fence on the other side of the field. Walk on to cross the River Trothy, by way of a footbridge under a very large tree, and bear right to go through a gate on the opposite side of the next field. Bear right up a faint grassy track and follow this well-waymarked bridleway along the left side of fields to a lane.

2. Turn right, joining the Offa's Dyke Path, passing "The Cidermill" before walking straight on along a stony track which climbs gradually up to and then through woodland.

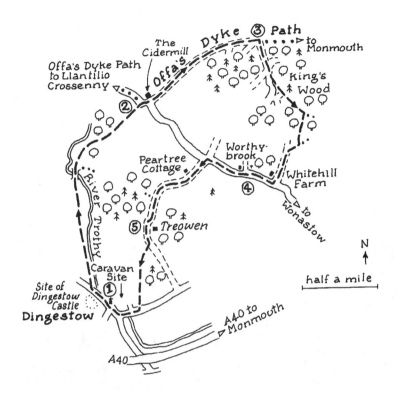

3. At a major junction of tracks and a finger post turn right up a broad forest track, leaving the Offa's Dyke Trail. Bear right at the next junction of tracks as waymarked and go straight on at the ensuing intersection, where there is a finger post confirming the right of way ahead. About half a mile after leaving the Offa's Dyke Trail, bear very slightly right along a faint grassy track, waymarked by a finger post, which soon diverges from the more prominent track. This track then narrows to a path descending through a clearing that permits a good view of the surrounding hills. Continue the descent through more woodland and pass through a handgate. Bear right down a field to go through the gate in the corner and turn left down a track past a farm. Turn right along a lane and, descending into a dip, watch out for the small Methodist church on the right by Worthybrook Farm.

This simple little chapel, built in 1850, is beautifully situated and still in use despite being isolated from any village community.

4. Continue along the lane to the intersecting bridleway and turn left down the track. Follow this track bending left before reaching woods to pass Treowen, a mansion which will have been visible for some time during this walk.

The present house was built in 1563, houses having been recorded on the site since Norman times. It was the seat of the Earls of Pembroke until the 17th century and is now opened to the public by arrangement.

Treowen: a huge 16th-century house

5. After passing a pond at the end of the associated farm buildings turn right through the second of two adjacent gates, as waymarked, and bear left to go through the handgate visible in the bottom hedge. Carry straight on to go through a handgate into woodland, turn right along the clear path and then right again along a lane past a caravan site into Dingestow. Turn right at a T-junction to return to the church.

Walk 20: The Kymin, Naval Temple and Staunton from Monmouth

Starting point: Grid reference 509128, car park by Monmouth School just off the A40 opposite to the Wye Bridge

Distance: 11 miles (17.7 kilometres)

Height gain: 1650 feet (500 metres)

Maps: Outdoor Leisure 14 (Wye Valley and Forest of Dean), Landranger 162 (Gloucester and Forest of Dean)

Facilities: Full facilities in Monmouth and pub in Staunton

Terrain: Mainly woodland tracks and paths for the first 7 miles and then riverbank meadows. There are three uphill sections starting with the steady but unremitting climb of the Kymin. The climbs to Knockall's Lodge and Near Hearkening Rock are relatively short.

Monmouth is a busy old market town with a wealth of fine historic buildings. The most notable is the 13th-century gated bridge crossing the River Monnow, the town being bounded on three sides by the Monnow and Wye. This fortified bridge, the only one of four at Monmouth to have survived, is unique in Britain and one of only three in the whole of Europe.

1. Cross the A40 by Monmouth School, using the subway, and the River Wye, by way of the bridge which dates from 1617, before turning left along the A4136 following the Offa's Dyke Trail. After rounding a sharp bend in the road, join the path inside railings on the right side of the road. Pass through two gates to bear left along a track and go straight on up a lane.

2. Where the lane bends sharply to the right bear left up a clear path waymarked Garth Wood and pass through Fiddlers Elbow National Nature Reserve. At a junction of paths, turn right over a stile and climb up the middle of a field following waymarkers to cross the stile in the top corner. Bear left along a lane for just 20 metres and turn left through a handgate back into woodland. Bear left at the junction of paths to keep climbing to the top of the Kymin. Turn right to the Round House and terrace, at a

height of about 840 feet, where there is a superb view of the Usk
Plain and Black Mountains with Monmouth in the foreground.

*The Round House was built late in the 18th century as a
banqueting clubhouse. The nearby Naval Temple was built in
1801 by the same club as a memorial to victorious British
admirals. Both properties are now in the care of the National Trust.*

Pause to admire the Naval Temple after the long climb up the Kymin

3. Go down the track past the temple and bear left through a kissing gate by Shortlands, signposted to Upper Redbrook. Pass
through another kissing gate and down the right side of a field.
Cross stiles to continue along an enclosed path and the bottom
edge of two fields. Bear right over a stile and turn left down a
track past a stone-built house. Continue down this track for a
generous half-mile progressively losing height.

4. Soon after the start of the tarmac surface and just before a sharp
right-hand bend, bear left down a narrow enclosed path leaving
the Offa's Dyke Trail. After a short descent, turn left along a road
for about 100 metres and then bear left up a waymarked path

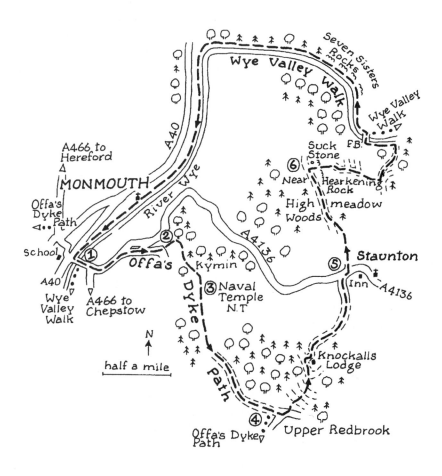

which soon turns away from the road to climb steeply through woodland. Cross stiles, the track bed of a long-disused railway and a forest track. At an intersection of paths, keep climbing increasingly steeply as the path narrows. Bear left along a forest track and turn right at a junction passing Knockall's Lodge. Walk straight on along this track for a generous half-mile, to the outskirts of Staunton, and go forward along the lane to the main road.

Staunton is an ancient Anglo-Saxon name meaning "the place of the stones". These mysterious stones in and around the village have names such as Suck, Toad, Queen, Long, Broad and Buck. The latter used to rock before it was dislodged in 1885 and was reputedly used in druid ceremonies. The early 12th-century church has a font said to be a hollowed out Roman altar.

5. Bear right across the road to pass along a waymarked path between cottages and veer left past the Well of St John the Baptist. This path to the next junction is a permitted route rather than right of way and therefore used subject to any Forest Enterprise notices. Follow the clear path through woodland, descending briefly then bearing right uphill as waymarked to contour along the top edge of a valley. At a junction of paths fork left downhill, as waymarked on a tree, and at the end of this path turn right along a forest track. Pass under Near Hearkening Rock and turn right, at a marker post under Suck Stone, up a well-worn path for the short but steep climb to the top of Near Hearkening Rock.

6. Walk away from the edge along a clear path and bear left across a forest track, to carry on in the same direction, along a waymarked path commencing the descent to the River Wye. Turn left at the first junction and fork right at the next junction of paths as waymarked. Cross a level track and continue downhill past a National Nature Reserve information board for Lady Park Wood. Continue descending at a crossing of tracks and then turn left down a permitted forestry track (see previous paragraph) to the river. Turn left along the track parallel to the bank, cross the suspension bridge and turn left along the opposite bank joining the Wye Valley Walk. This path is very clear, following the riverbank closely for the four miles back to Monmouth.

Walk 21: Clearwell Castle from Lower Redbrook

Starting point: Grid reference 536100, roadside parking by the telephone box on the A466 through Lower Redbrook

Distance: 8.5 miles (13.7 kilometres)

Height gain: 1150 feet (350 metres)

Maps: Outdoor Leisure 14 (Wye Valley and Forest of Dean, Landranger 162 (Gloucester and Forest of Dean)

Facilities: Full facilities in Monmouth, pubs in Lower Redbrook

Terrain: A firm clear track for the first two miles then field paths connected by quiet country lanes. The last two miles of the walk follow Offa's Dyke over firm, but sometimes rough, ground.

The tinplate works at Redbrook closed in 1961 being the last works in Britain to make thin tinplate by traditional methods. All trace of the works has now disappeared apart from the ponds, formed to drive waterwheels, passed at the beginning of the walk. This was also the last vestige of metalworking in the Wye Valley, which peaked in the 17th and 18th centuries.

1. Walk down the road towards Chepstow. Turn left just before the Fish 'n Game pub and then right up broad concrete steps, very briefly joining the Offa's Dyke Trail. At the top of the steps turn left along a narrow lane and, where the surface deteriorates, bear left along the major track soon passing a sign to "Glyn Farm & Glyn Barn". There are several ponds and a stream in the valley down to the left. At a fork in the tracks, signposted to Birt's Cottage, bear left and continue a very gradual climb up this lovely valley.

2. Pass the massive house at Glyn Farm, cross a stream and pass Birt's Cottage where the surface of the track changes to grass. Continue along this very clear track as the valley bends around in a half-circle past Lodges Farm and then bear left along a sandy track. Cross the stream and turn right at the next junction of tracks to cross the stream again and then bear left past a ruined barn. About 50 metres after passing the barn, before reaching the gate ahead, turn right up another track. At the top of the field bear left, leaving the track, and continue uphill crossing the next field diagonally.

There is a delightful view at this point towards Newland and its church. All Saints Church is known as "the cathedral of the forest" being the largest and most impressive church within the Forest of Dean. It is a principally medieval church dating from the early 13th century, whilst the village is also very attractive.

3. Cross a waymarked stile in the top corner of the field and climb more gradually in woodland. At the next junction of paths turn sharp right to climb out of the valley along a broader path. Climb a stile to emerge from the woods, then walk up the right side and along the top of a field to a stile just before a gate. Cross the stile and proceed along the partially enclosed path ahead. Continue ahead across stiles, a lane and two further stiles. Bear left down a field towards an old tithe barn, now converted into a house, noticing Clearwell Castle just visible in the distance to the right.

Clearwell Castle from the footpath entering the village

4. Cross the stile in the corner of the field to the right of the barn and turn left down a lane. Climb the stile in the high bank on the right when abreast of the barn and cross a field alongside the hedge to the left. Cross the stile adjacent to the stone wall enclosing the grounds of the castle and follow the wall to descend towards the ancient settlement of Clearwell.

Gaps in the hedge, replacing the wall, offer the best views of this early 18th-century Neo-Gothic mansion, which is not open to the public. It was built by the Dunraven family, also responsible for many other buildings in the village, including the church. The latter, completed in 1866, is in 19th-century French Neo-Gothic style. Notice the avenue of trees through the churchyard leading to

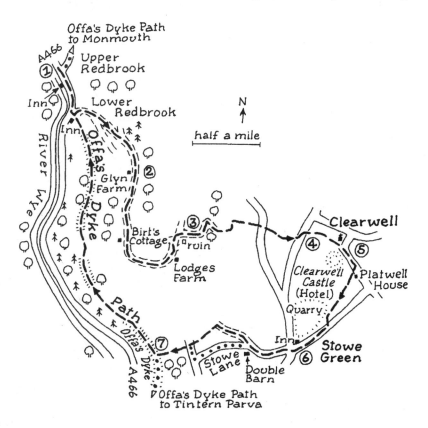

a private entrance to the church for the Dowager Countess Dunraven, who commissioned this particular building. Nearby are the famous Clearwell Caves where iron ore has been mined since the Iron Age, 2,500 years ago. These caverns are now open to the public.

5. Turn right along the road past the imposing entrance to the castle, away from the centre of the village and the famous Clearwell Caves. Just before the de-restriction road sign, turn right along a narrow enclosed path which may be overgrown for the first 100 metres. At the end of this path turn left across a stone stile and, 50 metres later, turn right over another stile initially between high stone walls. Continue in the same direction across fields alongside the hedge on the right, on the other side of which there is a massive quarry. In the third field bear left following overhead cables to pass through a gate and turn right along a lane past the entrance to the quarry.

6. Pass the Travellers Rest Pub, turn right by a telephone box and then almost immediately left down a narrow lane. At a sharp left-hand bend, by Double Barn, walk straight on along the enclosed waymarked path. (If this path is too overgrown to be passable carry on to the end of the lane and turn left to rejoin the main route of the walk at the finger posts on both sides of the lane). Cross a stile and turn left to follow the hedge along two sides of a large field. 20 metres before the stile ahead, turn left over another stile and go forward alongside a high hedge to the left. Bear right across a lane and continue in the same direction down two fields, increasingly steeply, enjoying views across the Wye Valley. At the bottom edge of a field adjoining woodland turn right joining the Offa's Dyke Trail.

The trail follows the line of the dyke, which for the most part can be clearly seen, to the end of Highbury Wood overlooking Lower Redbrook. Indeed most of the trail from Sedbury Cliffs to this point follows the line of the dyke.

7. Carry on through fields immediately above the woods, then briefly through the woods, and along the top side of fields passing Coxbury Farm. On reaching a marker post, bear right onto an enclosed path and into woodland climbing increasingly steeply. Bear right across a track and enter Highbury Wood, which is a National Nature Reserve. Continue climbing briefly before the path levels out and then descend progressively along the dyke. Leave Highbury Wood by way of a stile and turn left down a track, noting the old railway bridge spanning the River Wye below. Bear left at a marker post to walk down through fields and cross a stile near houses. Join a surfaced track to the concrete steps used at the start of the walk.

Walk 22: Bigsweir Bridge from Tintern

Starting point: Grid reference 537006, the Old Railway Station car park on the north side of Tintern

Distance: 9 miles (14.5 kilometres)

Height gain: 800 feet (240 metres)

Maps: Outdoor Leisure 14 (Wye Valley and Forest of Dean), Landranger 162 (Gloucester and Forest of Dean)

Facilities: Full facilities in Tintern, café and toilets at the Old Railway Station

Terrain: The River Wye is prone to overflow its banks in this area, rendering the path from Bigsweir Bridge back to Brockweir inaccessible. If in doubt, check the level of the river and take advice from the information centre in Chepstow or Monmouth. The alternative route of the Offa's Dyke Trail could be used, but it is a less direct path that will add to the height gain and directions are not included here.

The terrain is largely firm tracks and, in the latter part of the walk, grassy meadows beside the river. There is one short climb near the start of the walk followed by very gradual uphill sections to Pen-y-Fan, and the descent to Bigsweir Bridge. Waymarking is good as the walk utilises two long-distance trails.

The old station was restored by Gwent County Council as a tourist feature after closure of the Wye Valley Line in 1964. This line was constructed at a time when the valley was highly industrialised, enjoying the same advantages of river and woodland as Ironbridge. However, it ceased to be viable before the severe pruning of the railway network by Dr. Beeching in 1966. Old railway coaches house an exhibition about the history of the railway and provide tourist information.

1. Walk up the track bed past the old station building, joining the Wye Valley Walk, to Brockweir Bridge. Climb the steps to the road and turn left to the main road. Bear right across the major road to follow the waymarked path initially alongside the road and then winding uphill through woodland. The path is well used and frequently waymarked. Bear right along a clear track inside the top edge of the wood, climbing steadily through ma-

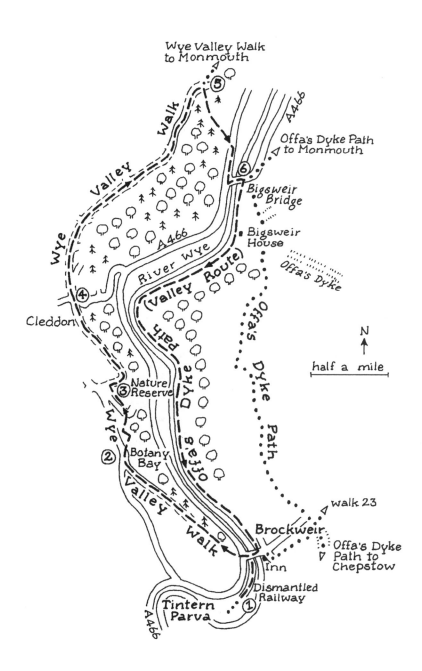

Wye Valley Walk
to Monmouth

⑤

Wye Valley Walk

Offa's Dyke Path
to Monmouth

A466

⑥

Bigsweir
Bridge

Bigsweir
House

Offa's Dyke

River Wye

A466

(Valley Route)

④

Offa's Dyke Path

N

half a mile

Cleddon

Offa's Dyke Path

Nature
③ Reserve

②

Botany
Bay

walk 23

Brockweir

Offa's Dyke
Path to
Chepstow

Inn

Valley Walk

Dismantled
Railway

①

Tintern
Parva

A466

ture woodland with views periodically across the Wye Valley. Descending towards a bungalow, walk straight on where the path bends left to a lane and then turn right.

2. Pass the large garden of the bungalow and bear right into woodland again as waymarked. Cross a stream and follow the obvious path inside the edge of the woods. Climb progressively and turn left up another lane for about 50 metres before turning right along another forest path. Turn left at a junction of paths by a picnic table to the Forest Enterprise car park and picnic site.

3. Turn right through the car park along the major track and fork left at the top end of the car park as the track climbs gradually along the top of the gorge, where there are some superb views. After the track bends sharply left, turn right at a T-junction where, for the first time, there are extensive views to the south and west. Follow a track that soon starts to descend between dry stone walls. Cross another track and carry on to Orchard Cottage on the outskirts of Cleddon.

Fishing on the River Wye

4. Cross a narrow lane and walk on as waymarked for the Wye Valley Walk and Pen-y-Fan. At a complex junction of paths, go forward as waymarked along a broad straight level track. Continue ahead, ignoring the footpath to Llandogo, along an enclosed bridleway which evolves into a surfaced lane passing Moor Cottage. Immediately after passing the driveway of Duke's House, bear right down an enclosed sunken path to start the descent to Bigsweir Bridge. Turn left at a T-junction along a broader track, then turn right down a lane past Spring Cottage alongside the spacious green of Pen-y-Fan.

5. At the bottom of the green, as the road bends left, bear right down a footpath as directed towards Bigsweir Bridge leaving the Wye Valley Walk. This path descends through mature conifers and then contours briefly along the bottom edge of woodland, before a further decent across meadows punctuated by marker posts. Cross a stile to descend steeply through woods and turn right along a lane towards the bridge.

6. Cross the bridge, noting the 19th-century tollhouse, and turn right over a stile, joining the alternative Offa's Dyke Trail, which clings to the bank of the River Wye down to Brocksweir Bridge. This route is obvious and well waymarked. It passes through meadows, along a track (take the right fork at a junction), meadows, woodland and more meadows before joining an enclosed path when within sight of the bridge. Cross the bridge and turn left over a stile to return to the old station by way of the track bed.

Walk 23: Hewelsfield and St Briavels Castle from Tintern

Starting point: Grid reference 537006, the Old Station north of Tintern

Distance: 8.5 miles (13.7 kilometres)

Height gain: 900 feet (270 metres)

Maps: Outdoor Leisure 14 (Wye Valley and Forest of Dean), Landranger 162 (Gloucester and Forest of Dean)

Facilities: Full facilities near Tintern Abbey, refreshments and toilets in the Old Station. Pubs and refreshments in St Briavels.

Terrain: A very gradual climb up tracks and field paths to Hewelsfield followed by a combination of tracks, fields, enclosed paths, woodland and quiet lanes and a very gradual descent from St Briavels. Ground conditions generally good but the lack of waymarking in places means that the route finding is not always straightforward.

Whilst the writer has not experienced any problem, the County Council reports that paths quoted in paragraph 2 have sometimes not been reinstated after ploughing. The County Council also advises that the path referred to at the end of paragraph 5 is prone to landslip when it may be impassable. Walkers may want to check with Chepstow or Monmouth information centre that this path is open though there is a lane parallel to the path about 200 metres higher up the ridge to the south. This lane is the same one as is referred to in the first sentence of paragraph 6.

Following the closure of the Wye Valley railway line in 1964 the old station was developed as a tourist feature in 1971 when railway preservation was very much in vogue. The line would undoubtedly have been very popular as a preserved steam railway but for the deterioration of the bridges and tunnels, which had made the original construction so ruinously expensive.

1. Walk past the old station buildings along the track bed and turn right over Brocksweir Bridge built in 1906. Turn right by the village pub joining the Offa's Dyke Trail. Pass to the right of Gregory Farm, which is a sanctuary for donkeys, ponies and horses, and then turn left up a track behind the sanctuary. Continue climbing steadily along this clear track, which is enclosed briefly after passing a large ruined barn (near which a finger post

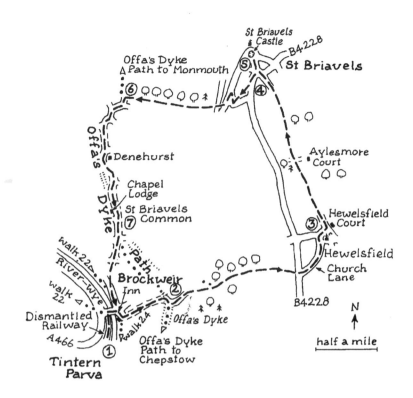

indicates an alternative route of the Offa's Dyke Path joining the track).

2. Before reaching the stile ahead turn left, leaving the Offa's Dyke Path, to contour along the top of fields, by way of a series of gates, on a faint grassy track. Pass a stile on the right, on the edge of woodland, and carry on alongside the woodland where the path is indistinct. Climb to the gate in the top corner of the next field, where there are good views back towards the Wye Valley, and bear left to contour across the ensuing fields through a succession of gates. Pass a water-cart and go through the gate in the corner of a field to follow a short track to a road. Go down Church Lane opposite into Hewelsfield.

This hamlet is grouped around the circular churchyard. The obvious unusual feature of the Church of St Mary Magdalene is the long stone roof extending to within feet of the ground. The church, with medieval features, is built on Saxon foundations whilst the nave dates from the Norman period.

3. Bear left around the church past the substantial lych-gate and turn left down the lane opposite the stile in the churchyard wall. Where this lane bends sharply right, turn left up a driveway as waymarked and then continue straight on along an enclosed path. Climb a stone stile, go forward across a field and then bear left to continue along the enclosed, and now sunken, path. Cross two stiles in quick succession and a driveway to join a broad stony track. Climb a stile and, at a crossing of tracks, bear left to cross a stile by a gate to carry on through fields alongside a sunken path; this is no longer the right of way and is impassable. Continue past two ponds and immediately after passing a white cottage cross the stile in the adjacent hedge to join a track into St Briavels.

4. Cross the main road and turn right down Pystol Lane, past the Crown Inn, to the centre of this old village where the castle, church and George Inn are grouped in a highly picturesque setting amongst old cottages.

St Briavels Castle, in the centre of the village

The castle dates from the 1131 but only the gatehouse and the 13th-century royal apartments are still standing, which are now being used as a youth hostel. The castle was the administrative centre for the Royal Forest and would have been regularly used as the King's lodgings whilst hunting. The very substantial church has a commanding view 650 feet above the River Wye. It dates from 1086 and, having been enlarged in the 12th century, was restored in 1860. The quaint old George Inn dates from the 16th century.

5. Walk back up Pystol Lane and go up the main road past an ornamental signpost. Turn right along a path, which bends left around the back of a farm, before crossing a field and stile to emerge onto a lane. Turn sharp right along an enclosed grassy track to a lane and turn left past "Gooseleaze". Turn right by a yellow water hydrant down a waymarked but well-hidden path to another lane. Bear left across this lane to go along a track for 30 metres and then turn right down stone steps, across a stream, to follow a well-worn rocky path. Bear left as waymarked at one junction and then right (not waymarked) to contour along a ridge in woodland for nearly a mile.

6. At a major intersection of paths turn left uphill, rejoining the Offa's Dyke Trail, and then turn right along a lane. At a junction of lanes bear left as waymarked and turn right at the next junction which, at the time of writing, is not waymarked (new signposting is however being installed in the year 2000 along this stretch of the trail). Bear left of the house ahead up a rough track and fork left at a junction. Turn right along a lane past "Denehurst" and then cross the stile on the left to climb steeply up a field behind the farm. Cross two stiles, continue uphill between bungalows, and then bear right to climb another stile and join a stony track. Turn right as waymarked down an enclosed path forking right at a junction to join a lane by "Chapel Lodge".

7. Turn left at a T-junction and go forward downhill at the next junction, leaving the Offa's Dyke Path. At a U-bend in the lane, continue downhill along an enclosed waymarked path. On reaching a lane turn sharp right along a track for 100 metres and then turn left down another enclosed path. This obvious path continues through woodland to emerge onto a lane to turn left into Brockweir.

Walk 24: The Old Railway Line from Tintern Abbey

Starting point: Grid reference 532001, car park adjacent to Tintern Abbey, though this may be full at peak times in the summer when the abbey is likely to be thronged with visitors

Distance: 7.5 miles (12.1 kilometres)

Height gain: 900 feet (270 metres)

Maps: Outdoor Leisure 14 (Wye Valley and Forest of Dean), Landranger 162 (Gloucester and Forest of Dean)

Facilities: Full facilities in the vicinity of Tintern Abbey

Terrain: A very easy start using a firm level track followed by a gradual climb of about a mile to the long-distance trail. The latter is generally a firm, undulating path continuing to Brockweir. Parts of the track on the last stage of the walk may be very muddy in wet weather.

The ruins of Tintern Abbey dominate the starting point of this walk. The walls and, in particular, the huge windows with their beautiful tracery are still largely intact. Building of this Cistercian abbey

Tintern Abbey: the renowned west window

started in 1131 and continued into the 14th century. The buildings have not suffered dilapidation to the same level as many other religious sites in Wales since the Reformation. A little way upstream is Wire-works Bridge, which carried a branch of the Wye Valley Line to the wire-works in Tintern, which closed late in the 19th century. It is now maintained as a footbridge and is utilised both at the beginning and end of this walk.

1. Walk down to the river and turn left along the track on the bank. Bear left past Quayside cottage to the main road and turn right. Immediately after passing the Abbey Mill complex, turn right along the left side of the entrance to the car park and cross the footbridge over the River Wye. Continue along the obvious path and turn sharp right through a kissing gate and field gate, as waymarked, to the riverbank. Turn left to follow the river downstream where there is an excellent view of the abbey. At the end of the meadow cross a footbridge, climb up to the old railway trackbed and turn right.

   The Wye Valley line closed to passenger traffic in 1959 and closed completely in 1964 having been opened in 1876. The building cost, even at that time, was some £30,000 per mile and the line never lived up to the expectations of the developers.

2. After about a mile turn left as waymarked up the more prominent path leaving the old railway track bed and then bear right at the next junction. Follow this track for the best part of a mile, firstly level then descending briefly before bending uphill, to climb out of the valley. Shortly after a sharp right turn, bear right across another path as waymarked, to follow a narrow path initially up steps hidden in the undergrowth. Cross a path, which is an old route of the Offa's Dyke Path, and continue uphill less steeply to a finger post by a forest track.

3. Turn left along the track, joining the Offa's Dyke Trail. At the point where this track passes through a dry stone wall turn right, as waymarked, back into woodland. Follow the generally obvious path along the ridge for approximately three-quarters of a mile. Turn right at a junction of paths, and shortly after, avoid

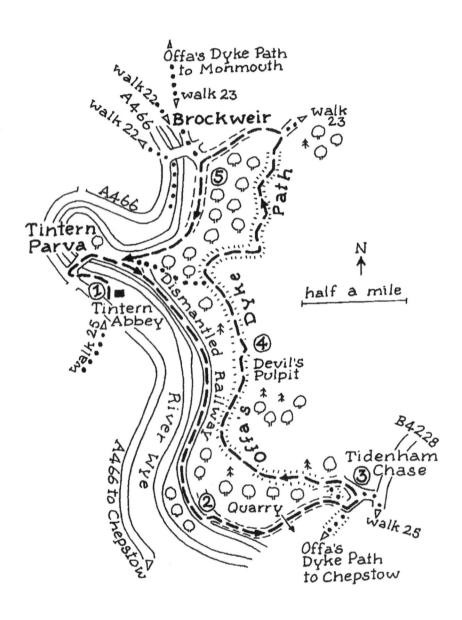

following a minor path ahead where the trail bears right up the ridge.

Pause at the signposted Devil's Pulpit, a rocky outcrop with a superb view up the valley to Tintern Abbey.

4. Soon after passing Devil's Pulpit turn left, signposted to Monmouth, to stay in woodland and at another junction of paths go forward waymarked Brockweir. Descend to another junction of paths and go straight on, later crossing a stile, and carry on along a level path. Bear left downhill as indicated by a marker post to emerge from the woods and turn left to another marker post where Brockweir Bridge is visible in the valley below. Turn right down the field towards the marker post in the bottom hedge, then bear right for 40 metres and turn left over a stile. Follow a clear track bending left downhill to Brockweir, leaving the Offa's Dyke trail.

5. At a T-junction of tracks by an animal sanctuary turn left, signposted to Tintern, and follow a broad track climbing and then descending towards the abbey. Bear left where the track passes through a gate to Abbey Passage Farm. At the end of an increasingly steep descent, turn right along the level path leading over the river to Tintern.

Walk 25: Tintern Abbey from Chepstow

Starting point: Grid reference 534942, Tourist Information Centre by Castle Dell Car Park – one of many in the centre of Chepstow

Distance: 12.5 miles (20.1 kilometres)

Height gain: 1650 feet (500 metres)

Maps: Outdoor Leisure 14 (Wye Valley and Forest of Dean), Landranger 162 (Gloucester and the Forest of Dean)

Facilities: Full facilities in Chepstow and in the immediate vicinity of Tintern Abbey

Terrain: Much of the walk follows the routes of long-distance trails which are generally obvious and firm but heavy usage creates some very muddy stretches in wet weather. There are three uphill sections of note, namely leaving Chepstow, Wynd Cliff after crossing the road halfway to Tintern, and between the river and Offa's Dyke Trail.

Chepstow is dominated by the castle which was possibly the first stone-built fortress established by the Normans in the decade after 1066. It was continually developed over the centuries and tested by the Welsh under Owain Glyndwr and twice during the Civil War, only falling into disuse in 1690. The Priory Church of St Mary also dates from the Norman Period and the finely sculptured West doorway has survived. The town gate at the top of High Street was rebuilt in 1524 having been part of the original 13th-century "Port Wall". In the early 19th century, Chepstow was the largest port in South Wales – partly due to the River Wye being navigable with goods being trans-shipped to and from ocean-going vessels. The advent of the railways and then the decline of industry in the Wye Valley, however, largely eclipsed this trade.

1. Walk up the park area to the left of the castle along a clear path joining the Wye Valley Walk. Turn right up the road towards the leisure centre. Turn right along the outgoing drive for the comprehensive school and leisure centre to the notice board giving information about the Wye Valley Walk.

Chepstow Castle from the bridge over the River Wye

2. Turn left to join an enclosed path and, passing through the gap
in the high wall, turn right. Follow the steps down to a viewpoint overlooking the castle and town before continuing along a
clear path. After about one mile fork right at a junction of paths
and, 60 metres later, pass through the Giant's Cave. After a further half-mile, climb relatively steeply up steps and converge
with the Monmouth road at a car park.

3. Cross the road and climb up the track opposite which soon
bends sharply to the left around the limestone cliff. Fork right, at
a division of paths, towards another car park immediately before which continue climbing by turning sharply to the right. On
reaching a bench where there is a good view of both Severn
Bridges, bear left, then proceed to a junction of paths by two
stiles and turn right uphill. Bear right down steps to a viewing
platform (Eagle's Nest) for a fine view over the Wye Valley some
700 feet below.

4. Rejoin the main path and bear left at a junction of paths by the corner of a field as waymarked. Turn right at the next waymarked junction of paths, near a stile at the edge of a field, and turn left 20 metres further on. The descent to Tintern Abbey starts with a steep rocky section and a rather boggy stretch using the obvious path. Climb a stile and bear left across a field as waymarked past a telegraph pole, where the next stile into woodland is now evident. Follow the clear path downhill, ford a stream and turn right down a rocky track beside the stream to the abbey, leaving the Wye Valley Walk.

This Cistercian Abbey, one of the loveliest and most complete in the country, was founded by Norman monks in 1131 and survived until the Reformation. At that time, the abbey's patron, the Earl of Worcester, only removed the lead from the roofs and the abbey bells so that the great church has remained largely intact. It is a superb example of the Gothic style with some of the elegant window tracery still in evidence.

5. Walk past the abbey to the river and turn left along a track following the riverbank. Bear left past Quayside Cottage and turn right along the road. Turn right at the car park entrance of the Abbey Mill complex and then immediately bear left across the footbridge over the river.

Wire-works Bridge originally provided the link for a branch line of the Wye Valley Line to the wire-works in Tintern, which closed in the late 19th century.

6. Bear right along the obvious level path and turn left at a junction of paths to climb steeply up a stony path signposted "Offa's Dyke Path 3/4". Fork right at the next junction of paths and bear right, then left at ensuing forks. At the top of a flight of steps cut in the rock turn left and then right along a level forestry track. Turn left at the next junction to continue climbing up to the Offa's Dyke Trail and turn right towards Chepstow. This path rises gently for a half-mile towards Devil's Pulpit, turning right at a junction of paths just before this point – a rock outcrop with a classic view up the valley to the abbey.

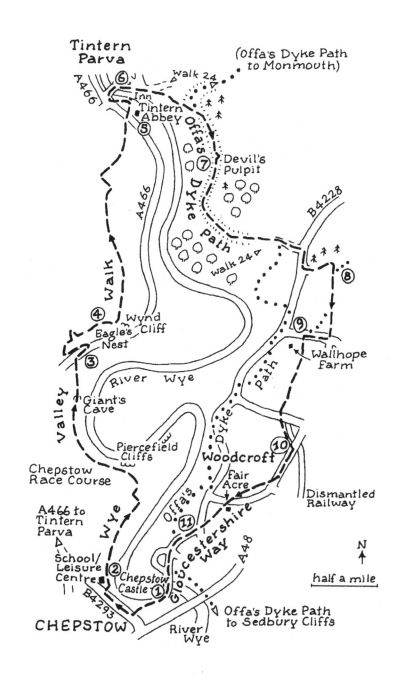

7. Continue along the obvious but rugged, and later improved, path ignoring the path to the left at the next viewpoint. Bear left at the next junction, as indicated by a marker post, and then turn left up a forest track where the Offa's Dyke Trail has been diverted. Turn left along a tarmac track, leaving the trail, and turn right along a road for about 200 metres to Park Lodge. Turn left down the drive for 10 metres and then bear right alongside the fence to join a clear path through woodland. Turn right at a crossing of paths and climb a stile to leave the woods, joining the Gloucestershire Way.

The Gloucestershire Way is another long-distance path running for 100 miles between Chepstow and Tewkesbury. The County Council advises that improvements to the signposting and the replacement of some stiles by kissing gates will be undertaken in the year 2000 as a Millennium Project. Such improvements are obviously welcome and should make it easier for walkers to follow this trail. This does not involve any change in the route but should be taken into account in following the ensuing instructions.

8. Carry on in the same direction down fields where a view unfolds over the Severn and the two bridges. Walk on between a hedge and an isolated stile to cross further stiles and emerge at a junction of lanes. Turn right up the lane past a letterbox and then bear left down a track towards Wallhope Farm.

9. Just before reaching houses turn left as waymarked over a stone stile and, after 10 metres, pass through a gap in the hedge on the left. Continue in the same direction over several stiles to the end of the hedge on the right where there is a marker post. Go over a stile by the second of two adjacent gates and continue in the same direction to the end of the fence, then bear right to cross a stile on the edge of woodland. Proceed down the track ahead and along the side of a garden to a road. Bear left across the road, cross two stiles and walk on alongside an overgrown disused railway track bed. Follow the hedge bending right to a lane and turn right.

10. Go through the next field gate on the right to walk alongside the lane, and then up the second side of the field to cross a stile. Carry on down a stony track; turn right over a stile, just before the track enters the farm ahead, and cross fields diagonally to a lane. Cross the lane by "Fair Acre" and two more fields, passing to the right of a small market garden, and climb over a stone stile at the top of the field. At the end of an enclosed path turn right along a street and then turn left down the road towards Chepstow.

11. Where this road bends left, walk straight on down Mopla Road – also used by the Offa's Dyke Path. Cross the road ahead and go down the path opposite, between high stone walls, to cross the bridge over the river into Chepstow where there is an excellent view of the castle. Halfway down the aforementioned path the Offa's Dyke Trail continues to Sedbury Cliffs, which is the starting point of the trail to Prestatyn.

Also of interest

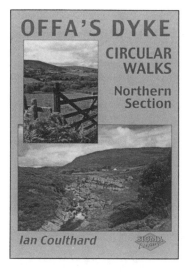

OFFA'S DYKE CIRCULAR WALKS: NORTHERN SECTION

Ian Coulthard

This is the companion volume to *Offa's Dyke Circular Walks: Southern Section*, and details another 25 energetic circular day-walks based on the Offa's Dyke long-distance trail between Prestatyn and Knighton. The walks average 9 miles in length and involve a height gain of up to 2000 ft. The routes incorporate many historic sites such as Valle Crucis Abbey and Chirk Castle. The guide also introduces walkers to delightful border towns such as Montgomery, Welshpool and Bishop's Castle.
Due May 2001
£7.95

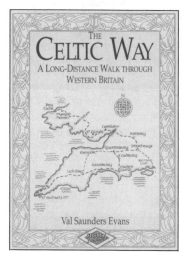

THE CELTIC WAY: a long-distance path through the sites of Western Britain

Edited by Val Saunders Evans

This pioneering 722-mile route through western Britain, including 400 miles of new walking, will challenge and inspire. The illuminating journey takes in Pembroke, Stonehenge, Glastonbury, Exmoor and St Michael's Mount. Tread in the footsteps of early travellers and settlers and visit 100 prehistoric sites including Caerleon, Avebury and Tintagel.
"Keen walkers will love the challenge presented by Val Saunders Evans " . TAVISTOCK TIMES.
£9.95

WALKING THE WAINWRIGHTS: with Stuart Marshall

Stuart Marshall

This ground-breaking book is a scheme of walks linking all of the 214 peaks in the late Alfred Wainwright's seven-volume Pictorial Guide to The Lakeland Fells. After an introduction to the Lake District, the route descriptions are clearly presented with the two-colour sketch maps facing the descriptive text - so that the book can be carried flat in a standard map case. The walks average 12 miles in length but the more demanding ones are presented both as one-day and two-day excursions.

£7.95

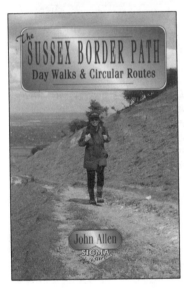

THE SUSSEX BORDER PATH: Day Walks and Circular Routes

John Allen

This new book is the ONLY guide to one of the best long-distance walks in England - the Sussex Border Path. Following the inland borders of the county from Thorney Island in West Sussex to Rye in East Sussex, it runs through 160 miles of unspoilt countryside with constantly changing views, charming villages and small friendly pubs offering good food and beer. The guide allows you to tackle the route either as a series of one-day walks (with its series of 26 self-contained route plans) or as a continuous expedition.

£6.95

All of our books are available through booksellers. In case of difficulty, or for a free catalogue, please contact:
SIGMA LEISURE, 1 SOUTH OAK LANE, WILMSLOW, CHESHIRE SK9 6AR.
Phone: 01625-531035
Fax: 01625-536800.
E-mail: info@sigmapress.co.uk
Web site: http//www.sigmapress.co.uk
MASTERCARD and VISA orders welcome.